To: Beverly

Merry Christmas

I love you,

Lisa Ferrante

2017

D050031?

$\int$P

THE
CHRISTMAS
Spirit

MEMORIES OF
FAMILY, FRIENDS, AND FAITH

JOEL OSTEEN

FREE PRESS

New York   London   Toronto   Sydney

FREE PRESS
A Division of Simon & Schuster, Inc.
1230 Avenue of the Americas
New York, NY 10020

First Free Press hardcover edition November 2010

FREE PRESS and colophon are trademarks of Simon & Schuster, Inc.

For information about special discounts for bulk purchases,
please contact Simon & Schuster Special Sales at 1-866-506-1949
or business@simonandschuster.com.

The Simon & Schuster Speakers Bureau can bring authors to your live event.
For more information or to book an event contact the Simon & Schuster Speakers Bureau
at 1-866-248-3049 or visit our website at www.simonspeakers.com.

DESIGNED BY ERICH HOBBING

Manufactured in the United States of America

1   3   5   7   9   10   8   6   4   2

Library of Congress Cataloging-in-Publication Data

Osteen, Joel.
The Christmas spirit : memories of family, friends, and faith / Joel Osteen.—1st ed.
p. cm.
1. Christmas—Anecdotes 2. Osteen, Joel. I. Title. II. Title: Memories of family, friends,
and faith.
BV45.O88 2010
263'.915092—dc22   2010032080

ISBN 978-1-4391-9833-9
ISBN 978-1-4516-0823-6 (ebook)

Writing this book has been a gift to me because
it's allowed time to reflect on all the Christmases
God has blessed with my family and friends.
This book is dedicated to those who've helped me
experience the full spirit of this holiday,
the birthday of God's own son,
our Savior Jesus Christ.

Contents

Introduction

✦

When we first talked about doing this book of Christmas memories, one of my family members said that I'd always liked stocking stuffers and this book is my chance to become one! I hope you'll find that it is stuffed with stories that inspire you, deepen your faith, make you laugh, and hopefully call to mind your own favorite memories of Christmases past.

Every family seems to have unique ways of celebrating Christmas. But what really hit home as we put this together was just how much Christmas is a celebration of family—God's family and our own.

God the Father sent His Son to us as the most precious gift of all. Jesus paid a high price to bring the promise of unconditional love, unending hope, and eternal life to every person who believes in Him. Once we'd gathered our favorite Christmas stories for this book and looked them over, we realized that without our planning it, each chapter contains those same themes of unconditional love, unending hope, and eternal life.

Faith in God provides us with those three gifts, and being part of a family helps us nourish them and pass them on from one generation to the next. Christmas is the perfect time to celebrate the love of God and family and to create memories that will last forever. Jesus is God's perfect, indescribable gift. The amazing thing is that not only are we able to receive this gift, but we are able to share it with others on Christmas and every other day of the year.

THE
CHRISTMAS
Spirit

✦

CHAPTER ONE

Our Father's Gift

We enjoyed the usual Christmas traditions growing up, but like most families, we had our own unique holiday rituals. The Osteen kids, all five of us, slept under and around the Christmas tree on the night before Christmas, telling stories and laughing and trying to guess what gifts we might be getting until we'd finally fall asleep. Still, we celebrated Christmas Day a bit differently from many families. For us it was really a big birthday party because my father and mother emphasized the holiday's Christian origins as the birthday of baby Jesus, God's perfect present to us. If ever there were a gift that keeps on giving, it was this one.

We did exchange Christmas gifts like most families. We laughed and carried on through huge dinners of turkey and all the fixings. One thing we didn't do, though, was eggnog. Instead, real early Christmas morning while our parents were still nestled all snug in their bed, the Osteen boys and girls climbed out of our sleeping bags and made home brew—coffee, that is. I probably should explain to you first off that caffeine runs in our family's blood. We were a coffee-drinking bunch before Starbucks ever ground its first bean. Every one of us started drinking it at a young age because of our dad, a pastor who started each day with a Bible in one hand and a mug of strong coffee in the other.

Dad's morning coffee was his little taste of heaven on earth. Each day, he shuffled out of bed and headed to the coffee pot first thing. Before he shaved, showered, or dressed, he had to down at least one mug of good old Folgers "mountain grown, the richest kind of coffee," as the commercials said back then.

Our father, John Osteen, didn't just drink his morning mug of coffee; he savored it the way my wife, Victoria, relishes Godiva chocolates. For him the best part of waking up was definitely Folgers in a cup. He really made a big production of his morning coffee.

I'm still not sure whether it was for his own enjoyment or for our entertainment; probably it was both.

I would sit with my older brother, Paul, and our sisters, Lisa, Tamara, and April, around the kitchen table each morning and wait for our dad to join us with his steaming mug. Watching our dad love up that very first sip of the day was a highlight of our morning, especially his first slurp. He'd put his lips to the cup, take a long, slow sip, and then hold the mug in the air with his eyes closed and a smile of contentment stretched across his face.

Finally, as we sat on the edge of our chairs waiting, Dad would take a deep breath, hold it, and let go a sound normally heard only from Saturday-morning cartoon characters.

Ahhhaaahaaaaaaaa!

We'd all giggle like crazy, and then each of us would take a sip of our own cups and chime in like the children's choir:

Ahhhaaahaaaaaaaa!

Without fail, Dad made the same deeply satisfied sound after his first sip every morning. We laughed each and every time as if it were our first viewing of our father's morning ritual. Do you know, to this day every one of John Osteen's grown-up kids makes the same sound after our first sips of coffee each day? Some of our own kids, members of the next generation, also have adopted the *Ahhhhhaaahaaaa!* coffee habit handed down from their parents and grandfather.

This is of course just a small part of the legacy left by my father, who passed in 1999. You are likely aware that he founded Lakewood Church, which he and my mother, Dodie, built up from a small congregation packed into an old feed store. As we've grown older and become parents ourselves, my brother and sisters and I notice more and more how deeply our parents' influence comes through in our daily lives in other ways big and small, on holidays and every day too.

Paul was talking recently about our dad and his coffee habit and how he would come to breakfast each morning in his thick terry-cloth bathrobe, shuffling along in his house slippers, hair a mess, sleepy look in his eyes. Dad would cinch that robe's belt sash tight and way up high on his solar plexus, making him look like he weighed three hundred pounds even though he was not overweight at all.

We often teased my father about how rumpled he looked in the mornings. Paul especially enjoyed doing this, but my brother admitted awhile back that as he was walking to breakfast one recent morning, he caught sight of himself in a mirror.

"There I was, in a big old robe knotted way up high on my belly, shuffling in my house slippers and my hair a mess," he said. "I realized I'd become our father!"

RISING ABOVE

Another Osteen family tradition handed down from our dad is at the heart of this Christmas tale. First, though, I should tell you some of my father's history so you'll get the full picture. Dad grew up on a farm outside Paris, Texas, back in the horse-and-buggy days. They didn't have television with shows like *American Idol* back then, but they did have singing contests on the town square on Saturdays, when the farmers and their families rode into town for supplies.

My father's sisters thought he should enter the contest when he was all of five years old. Before they took the buggy into town, they tried to fancy him up to look more like an entertainer. His thick hair wouldn't stay combed the way they wanted, so his sister mixed in some egg whites as a down-home hair gel to do the trick.

Unfortunately, the hot Texas sun beat down on Dad's egged head during the long ride into town. By the time he made it up on stage, the rotten-egg smell in his hair was so bad that instead of singing for the crowd, he threw up on them! Our father told us that put an end to his dreams of being a singer, and I'm pretty sure he stayed away from egg-white hair gel after that too.

In his younger days, Dad worked picking cotton on the farm owned by his father, my granddad Willis Jackson Osteen. Granddad was a successful cotton grower until the Great Depression. Like most, his family lost everything. They called themselves "dirt poor," but they lost even their land when the banks crashed and Granddad had to give up farming. He didn't give up on life, though.

Through his friendships with other farmers, he was

able to gather fresh produce, load it into his old open-sided truck, and drive into Fort Worth and Dallas, where he sold homegrown vegetables on the streets in wealthy neighborhoods. Still, times were hard, and Dad and his two brothers and two sisters didn't have much, growing up. My father often talked about going to bed hungry, having to put water on his breakfast cereal because there was no money for milk, putting cardboard in his shoes to cover the holes in the soles, and wearing hand-me-down clothes and pants that were too short.

BICYCLES FOR TWO

Despite the hard times, Dad had a mostly happy childhood. His family home had no electricity for the longest time, but they made the best of it. They'd sit on the porch, and Granddad would play the fiddle and make up songs. One time when my father was a boy, his sister Mary was holding him as they listened to music by the fire. She lost her grip, and he fell into the fire, injuring his fingers so they were scarred for the rest of his life. Music didn't seem to be a very healthy thing for my father as much as he enjoyed it.

Dad often talked about the fact that around the holidays his family was one of those to rely on charity baskets for Thanksgiving and Christmas meals. Most of the time, he and his brothers and sisters didn't receive Christmas presents. I think that's why my father later on took so much pleasure in buying us gifts himself. Growing up, we didn't hear a lot about Santa Claus. In part, I think my mother and father wanted us to stay focused on the Christian meaning of the holiday, but it also may have been that my father wanted to be the one to give us Christmas gifts because he received so few as a child.

Most parents sneak around quietly and buy Christmas presents, hide them, and then on Christmas morning tell the kids that Santa brought them down the chimney. Our father often took each of us Christmas shopping one at a time so we could help him pick out gifts for our mother and the other kids. It was funny; we were like Dad's little helpers on those shopping trips, but he never would allow us to carry the packages. He took so much joy in buying them that I think he just wanted to savor the feeling of carrying them to the car and into the house. Maybe that, or he was afraid we'd peek!

Early one December when I was about eight years old, Dad took me and April, who is two years younger, to look at bicycles. We didn't buy anything, and our father didn't say that day even who we were shopping for; we just looked at bikes together. A few days later, Dad pulled me aside and told me that he'd bought April a bike. I was really excited for her, so he took me out to the back patio where he'd hidden her new bike under a bedsheet. I wanted to look at it, but my father told me not to lift the sheet.

I was so thrilled for April, I went back every couple of days just to make sure her bike was still there. I asked Dad a few times if I could see it, but he'd say: "No, it's a surprise. You have to wait until Christmas."

I couldn't understand why he wouldn't let me see the bike, but I never lifted the sheet. I managed to stave off temptation, though I did keep an eye on the back patio to make sure April didn't wander out there.

The night before Christmas all the kids slept in

the den around the Christmas tree as usual. When we woke up around seven, Lisa put the coffee on so we could each have a little sip. Then our mother and father joined us, and once we'd all had our Christmas coffee and done the day's *Ahhhhhaaahaaaa!,* Dad said to me and April: "Let's go out back; I want to show you two something."

Finally, I thought; he wanted me to see April be surprised at her new bike, but when Dad pulled back the bed sheet, there wasn't just one bike. There was a purple Sting Ray girl's bike for April and a boy's cool ten-speed for me! I realized then and there why I wasn't allowed to pull the sheet back. Dad had bought a new bike for me too.

Needless to say, I was just as excited for me as I'd been for April! Maybe even a little more (sorry, April). My ten-speed was a fantastic bike, and the fact that it was my father's Christmas surprise made it all the better. I rode that bike for many years, zipping all over the neighborhood and cruising the cart trails of the golf course down the street.

When I think of that Christmas, I've often thought that my father's real gift to me was a test of faith.

God often works in the same way. He tests us without revealing His full plan for us to see if we'll obey Him and stay in faith just as my father tested me with that bike. Sometimes we don't understand why we are waiting. Often it is because God has something great in store, it's just not the right time.

THE GRAY BOX

One of our father's most special presents to us was the gift of a humble gray box. My father kept this metal container in a drawer in his desk at home. It was a very simple metal container, but that box and its purpose have taken on more and more meaning for us ever since the Christmas of 1998, the last one we were able to share with Daddy.

On a very basic level, the "gray box," as we always called it, was just the place where our father kept cash for us when we needed money and he wasn't around. There was never more than thirty or forty dollars in it, usually half of it in change. The gray box served as our private little Osteen family bank. That's how we saw it as kids anyway. Later, when we all had families of our own, we came to see that simple box as much more than a storage place for quick cash—our private ATM. We realized that it was a symbol of our father's love and caring and a symbol of security, created by a man who'd grown up without much, to assure his children that he would always provide for them what they needed.

Our father's love for us was unconditional and unlimited. We grew up drawing on that deep reserve of love, knowing that it could never be drained. As much as we took out, it was always replenished. God's love for His children is the same, of course. The depth of His caring is beyond anything you and I can imagine.

DEEP RESERVES

Our mother still has the original gray box, and I'm surprised we didn't wear out the hinges on the lid as we were growing up. Whenever we needed cash for school lunch, a pizza, a football game, or a class trip, or to go bowling or skating, our parents would tell us to go to the gray box.

When we look back now, it seems amazing that even with five of us drawing from it day after day, no one can ever recall finding the box empty or even short of cash. I don't remember ever seeing my father or mother put money into it, either. Yet the metal box always had funds when we needed them.

There was never a formal set of rules regarding withdrawals from the gray box, though there was something about its being for needs, not wants. If we were making a big withdrawal for some out-of-the-ordinary purchase, we'd leave an IOU note saying we'd pay it back or at least explaining what we were doing with the cash. The thing about the gray box was that it created this sense of abundance; this feeling that there was enough for us all to share in and that our father would always make certain we were taken care of.

Dad often said that his family never had enough and he didn't want us ever to feel that way. As kids and teenagers, we more or less took for granted that there would always be cash in the gray box. We didn't think about the possibility of its ever being empty, and that was what our father wanted.

Our parents had built Lakewood Church up to more than fifteen thousand members and a huge television audience. Dad was respected as a pastor who welcomed all into his church, which was widely known as an "Oasis of Love." This was a description of our family's church, which appeared on billboards all around Houston and was well known to people, but it was far more than a motto or slogan; it was a reality. My brother and sisters and I grew up in that oasis. His caring for us never let up.

Even after we'd all moved out and started our own families, he was always thinking of ways to reach out and assure us that we were loved and supported. As Christmas 1998 approached, Dad told Mom that he had a special gift in mind for each of us and our families.

"Dodie," he said, "can you help me find gray boxes for each of them?"

That Christmas, each of us—Paul, Lisa, April, Tamara, and I—received a gray box from our parents as a gift. With each of the boxes came this note typed on my father's old typewriter:

Dear Precious Children,

I know that you remember the Gray Box we used to have, where you could get lunch money or spending money whenever you needed it. Well, Daddy and I wanted you and your family to have your own gray box. So you could get money if you run out. We have stocked it—this time, but it is up to you to keep it filled up!!!!

We are so blessed to have children and spouses who have brought us so much joy through the years. Ones that respect us and honor us, and love us though we may have made mistakes through the years, and even though you still have fingernail scars from me pinching you!!!! Please have a great holiday season and a wonderful year 1999.

Much love, Mother and Daddy

I can't remember a Christmas present ever having such a powerful emotional impact on me—not even that ten-speed bike affected me so deeply. My brother and sisters and I have often talked about the thoughts that went through our minds as we each unwrapped the surprise gift that Christmas. It's interesting how similar our responses were. We each felt this overwhelming sense of being loved by both our parents and our heavenly Father too.

Lisa said that when she opened her present from our parents that day, she thought about how our father had always continued to honor God as he moved from an impoverished childhood into financial blessings. We serve a God who blesses and takes care of His people, and when we serve God and obey Him and give to Him, He will always take care of us.

Our father wanted to be sure that we each carried on the tradition of the gray box. We have done that, though we've all noticed it's a lot tougher putting the money into them than taking it out! My brother and sisters have embraced this family tradition as our father's parting gift. He left us with so much, but we are especially grateful for his legacy of love and security, the sense that in an often chaotic world that can seem uncaring, we are blessed with an abiding sense of being loved and cared for by our father on earth and, now, in heaven.

Dad had always been very active and healthy

despite high blood pressure, but then in the late 1990s his kidneys began to fail. Doctors put him on dialysis treatments, but they hardly slowed him down at all. He said he'd be preaching into his nineties, and we all believed that was true. Dad's faith in God was so powerful, and his spirit was so strong.

Just about a month after we each received our gray box Christmas presents from him, our father unexpectedly departed this earth. He died of a heart attack at the age of seventy-seven on January 23, 1999. We were not at all prepared for his passing, but thanks to his determined efforts, we were well prepared to carry on his loving legacy. We grew up living on the oasis of love created by my father, who taught us not only that we were blessed by God but that we should be blessings to others, because when we focus on that, God makes sure we are all blessed with an abundance of peace, joy, and fulfillment.

GOING HOME

A few months before my father went to be with the Lord, we drove back to Paris, Texas, where he was raised. Dad wanted to reminisce and show me where he had grown up. We visited the old homestead farm and the memories just came flooding back to him. He showed me where the well was and where he'd picked cotton and other sites from his childhood.

Then he asked if we could drive around to look for any of his old friends who might still be around. I'll never forget, driving up to this one run-down and weary old house, nothing more than a shack, really. An elderly gentleman was sitting out front on a log just passing the time of day. Dad went up to him, softly said a name, and asked if he was that person.

"I am," he said.

"I'm John Osteen," my father said. "We went to school together."

They hadn't seen each other for more than fifty years. They talked and talked about old times for a half hour or so before saying their goodbyes. Then we drove around a little more and found several more of Dad's classmates living nearby. All of them seemed to be barely making ends meet. One man about my father's age said he'd been laid off when he was twenty-eight years old and he'd never held a job after that. Most of them were on welfare and had no vision for a better life.

It seemed a shame. They were good people, but for whatever reasons, they'd never made their way out of poverty like my father. Visiting with them gave me an even deeper appreciation for all my father had accomplished.

It's amazing how one person can make a huge difference by committing his or her life to the Lord. When you live with integrity, when you dream big, and when you have a giving spirit, you can make a difference not only in your life but in the lives of others. My father touched people all over the world. He made a decision to rise out of poverty and defeat and a limited mind-set. As a result, he rose above his circumstances and helped countless others do the same.

My father's legacy was a Christmas present for all time. His message was for us to do good on this earth, to constantly be a giver, to sow seeds of love, seeds of encouragement, seeds of hope, seeds of healing, and seeds of blessings into the lives of His children and all of God's children.

CHAPTER TWO

Creating Christmas Memories

One of the highlights of our childhood Christmases was a big dinner with our Pilgrim grandparents. No, these Pilgrims didn't come over on the Mayflower or wear funny hats. *Pilgrim* was their last name: Roy and Georgia Pilgrim. They were my mother's parents, Texans born and bred. Salt of the earth, solid folks who worked hard, lived humbly, and always gave a helping hand wherever they could.

They weren't just our grandparents; they were like a second set of parents and a constant source of love and support for all of us growing up. Whenever our mother and father went off on a church mission or a vacation, Granddaddy and Grandmama Pilgrim stayed with us. Along with Christmas, they'd come four or five times a year, and we were always thrilled. Our grandmother would make wonderful meals for us. Our grandfather would mow the yard and fix things around the house and at the church too. He'd teach us to work with wood and on cars. He'd take us hunting and fishing, along with driving us to school, church, and all our games and practices.

Mostly, though, our grandparents made sure we felt loved. They were the most giving and reassuring grandparents we could have had. We were very, very close to them, which is one reason our annual Christmas dinners with them were so special. I realize now that one of the main things our parents and grandparents gave us for Christmas was memories. Not just memories of good times and holiday fun—sure, we have those too—but every holiday season and other times, too, they would share with us stories from their lives. These stories not only gave us a deeper sense of who they were, but their recollections also helped us understand who *we* are.

I encourage you to do the same for your children and grandchildren, your nieces and nephews, and all the young people under your care. On Christmas and throughout the year, share your lives with them. Teach them what you know. Guide them around the pitfalls that you encountered. And most of all, let them know that they are loved.

My grandfather was generous in passing down so many good things—his hunting and fishing skills, his mechanical abilities, his wise ways, his solid faith, his giving nature. Each of the kids in our family benefitted in some way or other from the shared stories of our parents and grandparents. It wasn't just their love and their stories that our grandparents shared. We were some of the most blessed teenagers in the world when it came to one particular gift they always gave us. Granddaddy Pilgrim didn't spend much on material things, but he did love his cars. He'd buy a new one every three years or so. Of course this was back when you could buy a new car for $3,000. His car-buying habit was a boon for me and my brother and sisters.

One Christmas when Paul was just about to turn sixteen, Granddaddy announced that he was preparing to buy a new car, so he'd be giving his "old car" to Paul. You know that our grandfather didn't exactly hot-rod around in his cars, and our grandmother didn't drive at all, so these hand-me-downs were like brand-new. On Paul's sixteenth birthday, Granddaddy Pilgrim tossed him the keys to his 1967 Buick Skylark. The sleek car was gold with a white roof. It didn't have air-conditioning or seat belts, but it sure beat walking. Lisa drove that same car when she was in high school.

Tamara and I shared another vehicle handed down from our grandparents. This was a green Buick LeSabre. We called it The Tank because it was so big, but we sure didn't complain. Well, I complained a little the time Tamara ran out of gas late one night during her senior year. The car died a few blocks down the street from our house, at the bottom of a hill. She walked home, woke me up at midnight, and begged me to help push home the tank with the empty tank. It was a struggle since neither of us was over five feet tall and 110 pounds at the time.

Our Pilgrim grandparents are both gone now, but we still talk about their generosity and kindness. I think of them nearly every day, and especially at

Christmastime because it's when all our family members come together, and I miss being with them. If you have or had grandparents like our Pilgrim grandparents, I know you, too, must appreciate them all the more this time of year. But if you didn't have the gift of a loving and supportive family, I encourage you to be that gift for someone else. It doesn't have to be a relative; it can be a friend, a coworker, or just someone you know who is alone or hurting over the holiday.

TIME AND
OTHER TREASURES

We tend to think of Christmas gifts as toys, clothing, or jewelry we buy, wrap up in paper and ribbons, and put under the tree for one another. But the quiet examples and soft places to land provided by caring people like our Pilgrim grandparents are some of the greatest gifts of all. The best we can offer others is the gift of our time. A helping hand, a listening ear, simple words of encouragement and support: these are presents wrapped in love and caring. They may be small gifts handed out just now and then, but over the years they add up to so much.

Scripture teaches that at every opportunity we should "do good to all people" (Galatians 6:10 NASB). I'd like to think that we all hold that in our hearts. Most of us want to be good to those around us, but this is the time of year when we should think about putting that thought into action, being proactive and thinking: *Whom can I bless today? Whose needs can I serve? Whose Christmas blessing can I be?*

Scripture warns that in the "last days" the love of the great body of people will grow cold (see Matthew 24:12 and 2 Timothy 3:1–8). I don't know about you, but I'm doing my best to stay warm.

Sometimes we might find ourselves dwelling on resentments we've nourished toward people who've done wrong by us. We might fall into harboring grudges and hard feelings for slights, hurtful words, or bad deeds. My encouragement to you is to put away for good those negative and unconstructive thoughts. Make this Christmas season the first of many seasons in which you accept gratitude as your gift. Think of those who nourished and encouraged you, and become a nourisher and encourager yourself. This is probably the best time to start with that new attitude, because this is the season of joy, the holiday in which we express gratitude for God's gift of His Son.

We all feel swept up by our own problems and concerns. It's easy to become focused inward, even during the holidays with all the things needing to be done. But this is also the time of year when we can make a big impact with little gestures. I'm reminded of this whenever my grandparents come to mind. They left their grandchildren with such a great and caring legacy.

We still talk about Grandmama Pilgrim's mouth-watering pumpkin, pecan, and mincemeat pies. But as good as those pies were, my grandmother's hugs were even more memorable. She was a bighearted, heavy-set woman with the sweetest, most serene disposition. When she hugged me, I felt like I could stay cuddled in her arms for the rest of my life. Grandmama Pilgrim was an Olympic-level hugger. Paul says being hugged by her was like being swallowed up by plush pillows. For a child, the sensory experience was almost overwhelming, because along with hugging you until you almost passed out from bliss, our grandmother always smelled like whatever sweet treat she'd been baking that day.

She was known also for making these sweet little sighing sounds under her breath as she worked in the kitchen, around the house, in the garden, whatever she was doing. Contented little sighs and peace radiated from her. She had a joyful spirit. When she spoke, there was always a trace of laughter in her voice, a quiet little chuckle trickling through the words. I can still hear her lilting laugh and her soft drawl: "Joel hon', what are ya'll doin'?"

Grandmama Pilgrim was a very traditional Southern lady who never went out in the sun and never took the wheel of a car. Granddaddy Pilgrim doted on her and waited on her—and waited and waited. She could take half the morning getting ready for church. His pet name for her was Slowpoke.

There was nothing pokey about our grandfather, though. He was one of those quiet, purposeful men who always had one or two or a dozen projects going in his work shed and around the house. An industrious person who knew how to build everything and fix anything, he relaxed by fishing and hunting. No one can remember him ever being idle.

There are two types of men: those who keep their spare nails, tacks, and screws in little glass jars and those who don't. Granddaddy Pilgrim was one of the former, very organized. Jar after jar sat carefully arranged, each in its designated place in a work shed that was as neatly kept as any you'll ever see. I still have a set of pristine socket wrenches he gave me years ago. I don't know that many people get sentimental over socket wrenches, but I do every time I see them.

Paul's the same way, maybe worse. Granddaddy had a sink in his work shed, and that's where he shaved every morning. Paul and I loved to watch Granddaddy Pilgrim shave because, as with everything he did, there was a thoughtful process involved, a daily routine honed to a science. Like most men of his generation, he used a straight razor and applied shaving cream—from a tube, not a can—with a neat little shaving brush. All I need to tell you about my brother's relationship with my grandfather is that Paul still has Granddaddy Pilgrim's shaving brush. He keeps it in a sealed plastic bag, and now and then he'll open the bag to catch a smell of it, triggering loving memories of their times together.

Our mother was an only child, and I think our grandfather saw Paul as the son he never had. Then I came along seven years later as a special bonus grandbaby! We were close, real close, but Paul had a very special relationship with our grandfather. Dad traveled so much in the years Paul was growing into manhood, and our mother's father stepped in and served as his mentor and guide. They became like peas in a pod, an older man and his young shadow.

Paul was taught to hunt and fish and maintain a car engine by Granddaddy Pilgrim, while our father was doing missionary work and I was still a small boy. Their bond grew beyond what is typical for a grandfather and grandchild in those times. My brother often talks with great love even about going deer hunting with our grandfather Pilgrim in the cold of winter.

"I remember the overpowering smell of bacon, eggs, biscuits, and coffee that he'd cook up long before daylight. And walking with him in pitch-black darkness through the forest, walking three-quarters of a mile to the deer stand," Paul said. "I was only ten years old and so scared of the dark woods on my own, but as long as I had my little gloved hand in his, I felt safe and secure."

Granddaddy Pilgrim grew up in the Depression years, and those of his generation who survived had the mind-set that they could lose everything in an instant but they'd survive somehow. They were a hard-working generation, determined, and loyal to family, because often family was all they had. My brother and my sisters and I benefitted greatly from the examples set by our grandparents and parents.

You know, Paul has a John Deere tractor like our grandfather had, and he said he named it Roy after "the hardest-working man I ever met."

"I am so grateful for the time I got to spend with him," Paul said. "He taught me how to hunt and fish, how to clean a shotgun, and how to clean a fish; he taught me how to saw a piece of lumber ('long, smooth strokes, Paul') and hammer a nail, how to change a car's oil and how to 'gap' a spark plug. Granddaddy also taught me how to be content with simple things: listening to the Astros every evening under his carport in those big clamshell metal chairs he painted every other year; he taught me how to enjoy a Coca-Cola ice-cream float and how to make homemade ice cream in a hand crank."

TRAGEDIES AND TRIUMPHS

Our grandfather learned all those skills out of necessity because he was orphaned at a young age and then cast out on his own. It is remarkable that he became such a gentle and giving spirit, because life was cruel to him early on. He's just another example that you can overcome your circumstances and rise above them. No matter where you came from, you can set a better course.

Granddaddy was just two or three years old when his mother died in a house fire started by fireworks set off by his brother. She was pregnant, and when she ran out of the house to escape the fire, she stumbled and fell, which caused her to hemorrhage, and she died. My poor grandfather, who grew up in Pine, Texas, had another tragedy just a few years later.

When he was eight years old, his woodsman father was working in the timber when he felt a sharp pain in his abdomen, probably his appendix. His coworkers took him to the Scott and White Clinic in Temple, Texas. He died there a few days later. The clinic sent a telegram to my grandfather's uncle, saying they'd sent the body back to Pine on a train, telling them where to pick it up.

My grandfather and his uncle hitched up a mule to a wagon and drove to the train station. They arrived at dusk, loaded the casket, turned around, and took my great-grandfather home to be buried. Paul and I often talked about what a sad journey that must have been for our grandfather. We'd imagine him as a boy riding all those miles in a wagon through the darkness with his father's body in the back. My granddaddy never forgot that lonely ride—the creaking of the wagon, its lanterns casting shifting shadows in the dense, humid forest, and the pine box in the back that carried the dashed hopes and dreams of his family.

There is still an eight-foot-tall memorial cross honoring my woodsman great-granddad in the cemetery there. It marks a tragic time in my grandfather's life.

Once orphaned, Granddaddy was passed around from one relative to the next for a while, eventually landing with an aunt and uncle. They had their own kids, and according to our grandfather, they treated him badly. He said they'd give their own kids money to go to town but make him stay and do his wash. They forced him to work in the fields while their kids went to school. He and his aunt clashed one day, and she came after my grandfather with a stick. My granddaddy reared up and defended himself. After that he was no longer welcome in their home.

My grandfather set out on his own at the age of fifteen. He joined a bridge-building crew for two years, working there until he looked old enough to lie about his age and hire on with a Humble Oil refinery. Then he set about building a life based not on what had happened to him, but on what he aspired to have: a life built on faith, family, and concern for his fellow man. He lived that lesson and imparted it to us at every opportunity.

"When Granddaddy and I stayed overnight in the cabin on hunting trips, we would get in our roll-away beds and turn on the electric blankets," Paul said.

"Then Granddaddy would take out his teeth, which made him talk differently, but I didn't mind. He'd tell me story after story of what it was like for him as a child, what his life struggles had been, how he dealt with the death of his parents, being raised with a mean uncle, having to leave as a fifteen-year-old boy—to be on his own. He also told me what it was like to build bridges in the 1920s—the heat, the physical toil, and the toll it took. He was tough as nails. One thing he never did was complain; he never was a victim. He was stoic, with tremendous resolve."

Granddaddy Pilgrim worked for the oil company for thirty-seven years, usually on the graveyard shift, and he always said he never missed a day of work. He built a little white cottage for $2,500 in Baytown, and my grandparents lived there for sixty years. I was always impressed with my grandfather as a boy, but my perspective has changed some now that I have a family of my own. I've seen what it takes to be a good husband, a good father, and just a responsible, God-loving person. Looking back, I had so many advantages over my granddaddy Pilgrim. Paul and I both had not just one good, loving, caring, and supportive set of parents; we had a backup team in our grand-parents. I think we never wandered far off the straight and narrow because there was almost always some-one there to gently steer us back.

Our grandfather became a good man with God's help once he decided to seek a better life. I can't imag-ine how hard it must have been for him to be alone at such a young age, to not feel the love and support that we mostly took for granted as kids. One of the great things our parents and our grandparents did for us was to tell them about their lives—where they came from and the people and events that influenced their lives.

This is another gift you can give at Christmas to your children and grandchildren, or to any young person who could benefit from your experience and even your mistakes. Share your life. Give them a deeper perspective not just on you but on life in this world.

When we gather for the holidays, the members of my family often talk about our parents and grandpar-ents and their histories. What's really interesting also is to hear the histories of our extended family members and to see that while we come from different places, many of our experiences are universal, especially our Christmas traditions.

Victoria's brother, Don Iloff, is married to Jackelyn Viera Iloff. Her family didn't come from poor rural Texas like ours. In fact, their background couldn't be more different. Jackelyn's ancestry traces back a couple of generations to Spain and the Canary Islands, but her grandfather Joseph Viera and her father, Jack, were natives of Cuba. Jackelyn's father was one of nine children whose parents owned a sugarcane plantation in rural Cuba. They also had a home in Havana, because Joseph Viera was a political leader in the 1920s long before Communism took hold of Cuba.

Jackelyn's father, Jack, and his brothers and sisters went to private schools in Florida, traveled often, and led a privileged life until the government was overthrown. All but one of the Viera children and their mother, Clara Rose, were sent to the United States for safety. Joseph and one son remained in Cuba to try and salvage their homes and businesses. Eventually, though, they too had to leave Cuba because of the revolution and economic instability. The Vieras lost their homes, their businesses, and their country. Revolution tore apart Cuba, and then wars caused turmoil in the United States and around the world.

Theirs was a difficult time, yet like millions of others, they persevered and built a new life despite challenging circumstances. They were not defeated. They stood together and met those challenges. Jackelyn's family moved to California. Her father became an electrical engineer for Pacific Bell Telephone. His mother, Clara, who lived to be a hundred and two, held the family together mostly through strength of character and an incredible capacity for love and understanding.

"Most amazing was her steadfast will to see her children succeed, her optimism, and her strong sense of duty and righteousness," Jackelyn remembers. "The kindness and generosity she always showed to friends and neighbors was deeply instilled in her children, along with her unfailing love of God and her utter faithfulness that He would bring them through all challenges."

Like our family and so many others, the Vieras kept the bonds close over the decades by celebrating

Christmas together. I know it's often difficult for far-flung family members to reunite over the holidays, but there is something very spiritual about this tradition. When Jesus was born to Joseph and Mary, they became a family, so it is fitting also to celebrate family on Christmas Day. I hope you will do that this Christmas. Take time to give thanks for your parents, grandparents, brothers, sisters, aunts, uncles, cousins, and all your extended family. But also share the history of your family with the younger generation so they can one day understand that they are links in a chain, part of something greater than themselves, and that they have a responsibility to uphold family traditions, values, and faith in God.

Jackelyn said the Vieras gathered for many years at her grandmother's house for Christmas dinner. Often there were more than fifty children, grandchildren, great-grandchildren, and other family members and friends. They would spend days preparing the meal and desserts that reflected their Spanish, Cuban, and American heritage. The elder members of the family told stories of their ancestors' lives and their own, passing on the knowledge that even those who've lost everything, including their countries, can survive and one day thrive.

There is yet another tradition passed down at the annual Viera Christmas parties. Each Christmas, Jackelyn's father would ask their church for the names of families in need. Then the Viera adults and their children would prepare bags of groceries and toys and deliver them. Jackelyn's father also made annual trips across the border to Mexico, taking bags and boxes of shoes, clothing, books, and toys for orphans. "This is how my dad honored God and praised Him for his life and the life of his family," Jackelyn said.

Jack Viera also was known for aiding relatives who'd fallen on hard times. He'd just show up and fix whatever needed fixing, while his wife helped clean what needed cleaning. They also chipped in financially with other relatives wherever there was a need in the family, helping with bills, groceries, and education expenses.

The tradition of family caring is one that sends out ripples that cause waves for decades to come. In Matthew 25:40 (NLT) we read: "The King will say, 'I tell you the truth, when you did it to one of the least of these my brothers and sisters, you were doing it to me!'" Jackelyn describes her family Christmases as "bountiful" not just in food and desserts and gifts but also bountiful in spirit. "It was the spirit of giving to others, the sense of family, and the thanksgiving to God that created the best memories," she said. "It is the best legacy!"

Jackelyn Viera's grandparents eventually lost much of their material wealth, but what they passed on to their children was a legacy richer than gold or silver—the understanding that blessings come in many forms, but the greatest of these is love. My Pilgrim grandparents were much the same way. Granddaddy Pilgrim never earned more than $15,000 a year. Yet he often talked to us about the importance of saving money, spending it wisely, and always giving whatever you could afford to those in need.

He passed that on to his grandchildren. I often say in my sermons that if you want to reap good things, you must sow good seeds, because the Bible says we reap what we sow. In 2 Corinthians 9:6–8 (NIV), we're told: "Remember this: Whoever sows sparingly will also reap sparingly, and whoever sows generously will also reap generously. Each man should give what he has decided in his heart to give, not reluctantly or under compulsion, for God loves a cheerful giver. And God is able to make all grace abound to you, so that in all things at all times, having all that you need, you will abound in every good work."

Granddaddy Pilgrim didn't just talk about the importance of giving. He lived it. He kept a little ledger book in which he recorded every tithe, every donation to charity, and every bit of money he gave to someone in need. For a man of limited income, he gave generously. His ledger book, which we still have, shows he gave each week to his church in Baytown and to our family's church in Houston. He was a cheerful giver, and God did bless him abundantly.

My grandfather worked all those years for a pretty small paycheck. He and my grandmother lived humbly. They gave freely but saved whatever they could too. Granddaddy took only a little of his paycheck in cash and had the company put the rest in a stock pension fund. The stock became Exxon Mobil stock and proved to be a wise investment. His retirement fund had grown to more than $1 million by the time he left the company. He told me once that his dividend checks were twice what his salary had been. That sizable sum gave my Pilgrim grandparents all they needed to be secure and comfortable for the rest of their lives, but they continued to live humbly, and their focus was always on helping others.

Granddaddy Pilgrim retired at the age of fifty-four so he and my grandmother could spend more time with us. If they weren't helping out at our house, they were lending a hand at their local church, my dad's church, or at a neighbor's. You could always find him mowing a yard, fixing a fence, or rewiring a room for somebody. He and my grandmother were most fulfilled when they were helping others.

I accompanied my grandfather a couple of years to the annual picnic and barbecue that the oil company held for its retired employees. I was always impressed by the regard people had for him and with the long-term friendships he'd built with his coworkers. Granddaddy, who was then in his eighties, would introduce me to a man of the same age and say, "We started working together when we were twenty years old and we're still friends."

Our grandmother Pilgrim died in 1997 at the age of eighty-seven, and the next year our grandfather's health went into decline. He was hospitalized for two weeks. We all visited see him when we could. Lisa went often, but I think Paul went nearly every night because he couldn't stand the thought of Granddaddy being alone. My mother arranged to get him out of the hospital and into home care, where he died peacefully, surrounded by those who returned the love he'd always given them.

I love the quote by John Bunyan that seemed to fit Granddaddy and Grandmama Pilgrim so perfectly. It says: "You have not lived today until you have done something for someone who cannot pay you back." I'd always thought it was a great quote, but when I learned about John Bunyan's most famous book, it gave me goose bumps. He was the author of *The Pilgrim's Progress*!

THE GIFT OF LOVE

My brother and sisters and I can never repay all that our Pilgrim grandparents did for us. As I said earlier, we talk about them all the time, and we especially remember them during the holidays because they were so giving and so loving. I guess you could say that their presence in our lives was the best present of all.

Scripture says people will know true Christians by their fruit (see Matthew 7:15–23). They won't know us by how many scriptures we quote. People will recognize we're believers when we live as my grandparents lived; when we're helping other people, meeting needs, and doing good works; when we're blessing people with our words and our actions. And remember, those blessings are multiplied, because so often they are passed on and on. They are like family heirlooms, Christmas gifts that never lose their value. Gifts that will make our family bonds all the stronger, for many years to come.

"Just as Granddaddy Pilgrim did for me, I take my

little boy hunting, and I hold his hand when we walk through the woods in the cold, long before daylight," Paul says. "I teach him to use a saw ('long, smooth strokes, Jackson') and how to change the oil in my tractor and truck. I still have my teeth, but I tell my children stories of my childhood and my granddaddy's too. The things Roy Pilgrim taught me in words and by example, about living and about life, will benefit my children and grandchildren as they benefitted me."

CHAPTER THREE

The Perfect Christmas

M y father founded Lakewood Church in 1959
and spent most of his life building and serving its congregation. But few people realize that early
in Lakewood's development, for about eight years in
the mid-1960s he left the pastor's role to spread the
Word of God in the Philippines and Mexico. Dad was
a leader in the charismatic-renewal movement, and he
was a sought-after speaker in those countries. During
that period, he was often out of the country on missionary work for weeks at a time.

My older brother, Paul, says he missed our father
so much in those days that he'd spend hours lying
in the front yard with binoculars watching planes fly
into nearby Hobby Airport, wondering if he was on
one of them. Other days he'd ride his bike to the end

of our street, Mustang Trail, and sit there watching for Dad's car.

"I'll never forget how excited I felt when I'd finally see his blue Chrysler Imperial coming down the street, realizing that Daddy was home," he said.

I was four or five years old the one year that our father couldn't make it home for Christmas. He was in India on a mission trip and missed his return flight. There were many sad faces at our house that Christmas morning. Our mother tried to keep our spirits up, but we could tell she missed him too.

Dad was a powerful, loving, and nurturing presence in our lives, so his absence left a big void. On top of that, he always took such joy in Christmas that he made it all the more joyful for us. He took each of us shopping for presents every year, and he was as excited as we were when it came time to open presents. When we learned that he was not going to make it that year, we only opened a few gifts, leaving the rest under the tree until he could join us.

The year our father didn't come home was not a perfect Christmas. We all carry around our own visions of the ideal holiday, don't we? We dream of spending the holidays with loved ones gathered around, talking, laughing, catching up, and sharing words of encouragement and support. I'd guess that nearly every spiritual person's vision of a perfect Christmas would include some time for prayer and worship, along with the usual exchange of gifts and big family gatherings.

Not having Dad home that holiday made us all aware, probably for the first time in our lives, that there is no guarantee of a perfect Christmas year in and year out. It was kind of a shock. We were a little spoiled in that way, I guess. We were so blessed to have our family all together, and we always got along so well.

EXPECT CHRISTMAS JOY

As my brother and sisters and I grew older, we realized, of course, that many people face less than perfect Christmases every year—soldiers away from their families, parents who can't be with their children, anyone separated from loved ones or going through hard times because of illness, a lost job, or a troubled relationship.

Sometimes the holidays have a hard time living up to our expectations. We set the bar high, and if things don't go as we'd hoped, we're disappointed. That's only natural, to some degree. You may find it helpful in those times to think about the original Christmas Day, the birthday of Jesus, and just how humble that was. Joseph and Mary probably didn't think that manger was the perfect place for their child to be born. I'm sure they weren't thrilled at having livestock around. But look at what a perfect Christmas that turned out to be: a Christmas for all time. More than two thousand years later, we are still celebrating Christmas.

SHARE THE JOY

My father always helped our mother make our Christmases wonderful even though he didn't have such great holidays as a boy. He didn't feel sorry for himself. Instead, he tried to give us better than what he had. Dad often told us that the highlight of his childhood Christmases was receiving the food baskets donated to the poorest families in his town. He said the turkey and fixings that came in the annual holiday charity basket provided one of the best meals he'd have all year. Because the Christmas basket was such a blessing in his childhood, my father created a holiday-basket program at Lakewood Church that fed hundreds of families each year.

Everyone in our family helped our church members prepare and hand out the baskets. Often, more people would show up for baskets than had signed up to receive them, but somehow we always seemed to have enough to give a basket to everyone who stood in line. We thought of it as our little Christmas miracle.

Lakewood's holiday-basket program was created as the direct result of my father's imperfect Christmases. As a poor child who grew up during the Depression, he had strong empathy for and a driving need to help others. People seemed to sense it too. I can't tell you how many times some stranger in need came out of nowhere and walked up to Dad as if guided to him by a heavenly hand. I was about fifteen years old or so and traveling with my father overseas during our Christmas break when I witnessed one of those encounters. We were on an island in the Philippines. The airport had a terminal with a thatched roof. I came back from the concession stand and found my father talking to a young hippie-looking guy with long hair and a backpack. They were having this deep conversation, which wasn't unusual because Dad liked people in general and enjoyed hearing their stories.

The next thing I knew, though, my father was reaching for his wallet. He pulled out a handful of money—he later told me it was a couple of hundred dollars—and gave it to the young man.

"What was that all about?" I asked when he returned to our seats in the airport terminal.

"We got to talking, and he told me he was trying to get back to the States but had miscalculated how much money he needed, and he was stuck here," Dad said. "So I gave him enough to get him home to his parents for the holidays. I just kept thinking, *What if he were my son or daughter; wouldn't I want someone to help him?*"

That's the way my father lived. He carried the Christmas spirit around with him everywhere he went, and people could sense it. He didn't have a lot of joy as a child, but he seemed determined to spread as much of it around as he could later in life. His boyhood Christmases were pretty sparse by most standards, but out of his imperfect childhood holidays, he created better days for others with his generosity, his spirit, and his caring nature.

Our Christmas without our father made us aware of how other people sometimes felt lonely or lost over the holiday. As kids, we may have taken for granted that we had two parents who were always there for us. That one Christmas also gave us a deeper appreciation for our father, what he meant to us and all he did for us. In some ways I think we all grew closer that Christmas because we realized, more than ever, the importance of family.

SADNESS TURNS TO JOY

You also could say that our first imperfect Christmas prepared us for others that would come. My sister Lisa was in her early twenties when she went through a divorce that left her lonely, hurting, and faced with a very difficult holiday. Now, Lisa wasn't alone and she knew that. We were all there for her, encouraging her and trying to cheer her up. But most people know what it is like to be hurting inside so badly that even when you are in a room full of loving and caring friends and family, you can still feel hurt and lonely.

When you are experiencing that sort of pain, remember that nothing can separate you from the love of God. The Bible says we are more than conquerors through Him who loves us. "No power in the sky above or in the earth below—indeed nothing in all creation will ever be able to separate us from the love of God that is revealed in Christ Jesus, our Lord" (Romans 8:39).

We told Lisa then that we were there for her and that God, too, was always there through the darkest nights and coldest winds. Sometimes we need to remember that in our neediest times God pulls us closer, so close that while we may not be able to see Him, we can know He is there.

Lisa spent the morning with us that Christmas, but she also took some time away from family. She wanted to take the focus off her troubled heart. She remembered how my father had taken the imperfect Christmases of his childhood and used them as inspiration to make the holidays better for others.

Lisa had helped put together Christmas charity baskets at Lakewood over the years. She'd always felt good making them and handing them out. That Christmas she decided that on this less than perfect Christmas for her, she would do what she could to make the day a little better for others experiencing rough times. She went to a Houston shelter for the homeless and worked in the soup kitchen for half the day and part of the night.

"I'd learned that one of the greatest things I could do when my situation wasn't the best was to reach out to others and meet their needs," she said. "I wasn't feeling blessed, so I thought I should be a blessing to others."

Lisa was moved by the experience of serving men and women living on the streets in complete poverty. Like my father, she kept thinking that they were someone's sons and daughters, someone's brothers and sisters, whose lives had been torn apart by tragedy, hard times, or dependency. Serving them, she turned her focus away from what she'd lost and put it on what she had to give.

The Bible says if you share your food with the hungry and provide shelter to the poor "your light will break forth like the dawn and your healing will quickly appear." Just as my father's imperfect Christmas made him more aware of the needs of others, Lisa, too, took the opportunity to reach out to other burdened souls on her less than perfect day.

CHRISTMAS IN REHAB WITH THE GRINCH

My friend Matthew Barnett had an experience similar to Lisa's. Matthew is senior pastor for a great church, The Dream Center, in the inner city of Los Angeles that serves the homeless, addicts, and others who need God in their lives. You can imagine that their Christmas Days are far from perfect, yet Matthew told me that one of the most memorable holidays he's ever had was spent with a group of men in a drug rehabilitation program.

Many were still in difficult detoxification programs. Most had nowhere else to go for Christmas. Their families and friends had given up on them. The men Matthew chose to spend his Christmas Day with finally had looked to God for their salvation. They had been studying Scripture, but hope was still hard for them to grasp.

This sounds like a sad scene, but into that dark setting a ray of light was provided when the people running the rehab center turned on a great movie that Christmas morning: *How the Grinch Stole Christmas.*

At first Matthew wondered how these depressed and despairing men would respond to the classic holiday cartoon movie taken from the work of children's author Dr. Seuss. He thought they might find it silly or childish, given their grim situations.

Instead, they responded to it like men starved for laughter and love, Matthew said.

"The movie experience was funny because the men in rehab were so new in their passion for God, that they were relating everything in the movie back to their newfound hope in Christ and to their old struggles," the pastor said. "In the touching scene when the

Grinch's heart got bigger one of the guys shouted out, 'The Grinch found Jesus!'"

Only a few minutes into the movie, the rehab center was echoing with an unfamiliar sound, that of grown men laughing and carrying on like carefree children, saying amen to each other's joking comments and one-liners, even crying quietly when the Grinch was cast aside, and then celebrating his comeback with cheers.

"They were not just watching a movie; they were watching it through the eyes of their own pain, their own loss, and their own triumph back into life again," Matthew said.

The pastor wept along with them when he saw the joy they found in simply watching a movie because he said it wasn't like they were watching a movie, it was more like they were having a revival meeting. They were reviving their spirits, letting some joy into their lives again.

Matthew said one of the men laughing and carrying on during the movie had lived under a bridge for seventeen years. Another had lost his family because of his addiction. One former heroin addict leaped to his feet with his Bible in hand, cheering the Grinch and telling him to keep on preaching when the character turned his life around in the movie's plot.

After the movie, the mood in the rehab center was dramatically changed. The residents laughed and talked of Jesus and the lessons they'd learned from the Grinch's journey out of the darkness and into the light. Matthew said that most of those men had lost everything. They could have remained bitter and angry and without hope, but on that Christmas Day, he saw God at work in their lives.

Matthew said that day ranks as one of the best Christmas Days in his life, the day he spent his holiday in rehab with the Grinch.

"I'd gone into that day wanting to inspire them, encourage them, and lift them up," he said. "But it was the pastor and the teacher who was inspired by them instead. That Christmas was special and not even one gift was exchanged. My gift on that day was the gift of perspective."

As Matthew witnessed, it really doesn't matter how much you have lost, how much you regret, how many times you've thrown in the towel. When you have Jesus in your life, you have everything. Having the hope of Jesus is all that you need to turn your life around.

FAITH, HOPE, AND FAMILY

Loneliness and heartache can burden any one of us, and the holidays often seem to make the pain feel greater. Our brother Paul said he'll never forget another holiday when he was feeling terribly lonely. He was single after a breakup. He'd tried to distract himself by starting a building project in his backyard with a friend. His buddy asked innocently, "Have you got any plans for the holiday?"

Paul didn't respond, because he had no plans and the thought of it just made him feel lonelier, so "just like men do, I kept on hammering and sawing and trying to bury my pain." He was still working away when the UPS man came walking around from the front of the house. He was carrying a big box of Paul's favorite candy and with it a note from our little sister Tamara, whose family nickname is Roo-Roo.

"I love you and miss you. Have a happy holiday," her note said.

Paul recalls that those were the sweetest chocolates in one of the most bitter times of his life, because they reminded him that he was not only worthy of love, but truly loved. Roo-Roo's surprise gift was a small, thoughtful gesture that caused a big shift in Paul's perspective. She revived the spirit of the holiday for him.

My brother always teases that when I was born, my "happy thermostat" was set at 99 while his was set at 15. The truth is that Paul is a thoughtful and caring physician and surgeon who works so hard that sometimes he feels run-down and overwhelmed. I'm sure you've felt the same way at times. You grow so tired you can hardly lift your arms, let alone your spirits.

One year at Christmastime, Paul was working as a family doctor in Little Rock. He was married by then, with three little kids, and, you know how it is, he wasn't sleeping a lot between babies' needing their diapers changed and emergencies at the hospital. It wasn't a perfect Christmas season at that point because Paul just couldn't get into the spirit of the holidays. He was tired. Worn down.

Then just a few days before Christmas, an elderly woman, Ella, came in for a checkup. She'd had some minor operation. Paul had known her for years, and he knew she'd lost her husband a short while earlier. He expected Ella to be sad and still grieving, but instead she had this "peaceful stillness" about her, my brother said.

"She just seemed to emanate serenity," Paul recalled.

Now, Paul was on a busy schedule that day. He was running late for an operation scheduled for another patient. He found himself rushing through Ella's checkup, and as he was finishing up, Paul could tell that she wanted to talk to him about something.

He was surprised when the subject wasn't her ailments or concerns. Instead, it was him.

"Dr. Paul, how are you doing?" she asked.

Paul took a breath and apologized for seeming rushed. He explained that he was running hard between responsibilities with his babies at home and his patients at work.

"I just wish I had more time for them all," Paul said, and then, to be polite, he added: "Ella, is there anything you wish for these days?"

She studied him a minute, and Paul saw a light come into her eyes.

"Dr. Paul, I would give anything to be where you are now as a young parent," she said. "I'd give anything to hear the pitter-patter of little feet, to change a diaper or to make formula for my babies again. I miss that so much."

The wise woman reset Paul's clock that Christmas. She reminded him that he should slow down, live in the moment, enjoy and be grateful for every minute as a parent.

"She told me that one day I would look back and fondly miss the very things I was struggling to rush through—being a father and caring for my family," he said. "I realized I was living the best days of my life then and there and that I needed to appreciate them as they happened."

We all feel overworked and overwhelmed now and then. But you should be careful about your life becoming so busy that you miss the joys of living. Remember, God never told us to just be busy. He told us to be fruitful instead. Be mindful and take prayerful inventory of the activities in your life. Invest only in those that bring you joy and peace. Do that, and you will experience God's abundant blessing in every area of your life! His wise patient helped Paul realize something that we all need to remember not just on Christmas Day but every day, whether perfect or imperfect. Like the Psalms say: "This is the day the Lord has made; let us rejoice and be glad in it."

NEW BIRTH AND NEW PIES

Like many people who face hard times over the holidays, Gabriela was finding it difficult to rejoice as the Christmas of 1992 approached. She'd had a long walk of faith since her marriage fell apart.

The marriage ended shortly after she and her husband had purchased their first home and moved in with their two daughters both under the age of six. Heartbroken and despondent, Gabriela didn't know how she could keep the house and support her children. She also wondered if any man would ever love her and her children.

At first this newly single mother let the negative

voices drive her into despair. When her daughters visited their father on weekends, Gabriela stayed home with the drapes closed, drinking alcohol and smoking cigarettes. She was headed down a bad path. Gabriela did not want to tell her parents or other family members of her separation, so she isolated herself from them just when she most needed their love and support.

As the holidays approached, she received notice of foreclosure on her home. The bank also was threatening to repossess her car. Her former husband had handled all the finances. Gabriela had no idea what to do. Her paycheck was barely covering the utility bills and weekly groceries. At one point she found herself frantically searching for matching socks for her youngest child because she didn't have money enough for new ones.

Gabriela had always been a joyful, talkative, and fun-loving person. But the breakup of her marriage and her financial problems left her dispirited and in despair. In her darkest moments, she had thoughts of suicide.

One of her coworkers tried to reach her, sharing Scripture and encouraging Gabriela to ask for God's help. She invited Gabriela to church one Sunday. They came to Lakewood, where my father welcomed and encouraged Gabriela. She'd learned as a child that Jesus died on the cross, but she had never understood the depth of pain He'd endured for our sins. When she learned of His suffering, Gabriela felt she owed Him the best life she could create.

That November of 1992 she accepted the Lord as her Savior. Such a feeling of relief and gratitude came over her that she promised my father that she would dedicate a year of her life to Lakewood. She lived up to that promise. My dad used to say that whenever he opened the church doors, there she was, waiting to walk in, drop to her knees, and pray.

Gabriela found a sense of peace at Lakewood. God's presence in her life renewed her spirit and gave her strength. She cried through her first week or two of services. Looking back, she remembers thinking, *God is cleaning me up, washing me from the inside out.*

She realized that she and her daughters were loved not only by her family but by their Father in heaven. One day in church, Dad offered a message of hope, and Gabriela says she felt so strong, she could conquer the world. The more she heard from Scripture, the more she hungered for God's Word. She read the Bible in every spare moment and decided to change her life for the better, one day at a time.

Gabriela had turned a corner, but Christmas Day was approaching, and she still had no money and no way to give her children the Christmas she felt they deserved. She surrendered it to God, trusting in her newfound faith. Then just a week before Christmas, her brother and his wife called.

"We want to take you Christmas shopping for the girls," her brother said. "It's on us."

Gabriela's brother was not a wealthy man. He had a child of his own. But he wanted to help his sister in her time of need. Scripture says if you seek the kingdom of God above all else and live righteously, He will give you everything you need (see Matthew 6:33). The Lord provided for Gabriela. She and her brother and sister-in-law went Christmas shopping and bought a house for her daughters, a fully furnished dollhouse. Gabriela wrapped every single piece of furniture separately so her girls could experience the joy of unwrapping each one.

"The girls had all these gifts to open, and that in turn brought me great joy to see their happy faces," she said. "I believe that is how the Lord feels when He gives us what we want. He is a good Father who wants to bless us. He says in Philippians 4:19 that 'God who takes care of you will supply all your needs from His glorious riches, which have been given to us in Christ Jesus.'"

Today Gabriela is the staff photographer at Lakewood Church. She is remarried with four children and once again full of joyous enthusiasm. When things looked dark for her, she stumbled at first, but then, as she says, "I ran to God, and I'm on my way to heaven and have true peace and joy. God wants to bless us exceedingly abundantly above all that we can ask, think, or even imagine."

You may be looking at a holiday season that seems less than perfect right now, but I encourage you to focus not on what is missing, but on what is there; not on what you lack, but on what you have; not on what you wish you had, but on what you actually have. Rejoice and be glad for the day the Lord has made, and make it as perfect as you can!

If you do that, you might be surprised with what happens. You might just end up having a much better Christmas than you dreamed possible. The truth is, as much as you might plan for the perfect holiday, only God can create perfection. Sometimes, His vision of perfect may be different from yours. He may have an entirely different path to the perfect Christmas than the one you had in mind.

Sheila, who is part of our publishing team, discovered the truth of that just a few Christmases ago. She was in charge of bringing desserts for two parties, a Christmas Eve dinner for her family and a Christmas Day meal with her husband's family. Twenty people had put in their pie orders for those meals. Sheila is a very organized person, so a week before Christmas she ordered seven pies—two pecan, two pumpkin, two chess, and one lemon meringue—from her favorite bakery in Dallas, where she lives.

Sheila had many errands to run on Christmas Eve day, so she and her mother, Anna, planned on picking up the pies late that afternoon. They had not planned on Dallas being socked by a freak blizzard that same day. The mother and daughter made it through rain, sleet, and snow to the bakery just before it closed early for the holiday. But when they walked into the place, Sheila felt a rush of panic.

Usually every display case and shelf in this bakery was loaded with pies, cakes, cookies, and pastries. All Sheila saw were crumbs, and there weren't many of them scattered around. Her fears weren't eased any by the two teens behind the counter. They didn't seem the least bit interested in helping Sheila in her moment of pie panic. In fact, they appeared to be trying to sneak out just as she and her mother walked in.

When they saw the two customers come through the door, the teens ducked into a back room. After a minute or two, one of them came out of hiding, but he refused to wait on them, busying himself with a broom instead.

Finally he looked up at them and said: "Sorry, ladies, we're sold out."

Sheila then handed him the receipt for her seven-pie order. He shook his head and said: "We have no record of this order, sorry."

Visions of a dozen empty dessert plates and as many disappointed children danced in Sheila's head.

"I ordered seven pies. I have my receipt. How can you tell me you have no record?" she demanded.

No reply from the kid behind the counter. Sheila told him that she and her mother weren't budging until they had their pies.

It was a standoff in the pastry section.

Another customer had walked in from the cold during the heated exchange. In the spirit of the holidays, she tried to promote peace on earth, or at least in the bakery.

"I'm going to pray that you'll find some Christmas pies," she said to Sheila and her mother.

Sheila glared at her, thinking, *We don't need prayer. We need pies!*

"I know prayer works," said the woman, holding her higher ground.

Sheila and Anna trudged pieless back out to their car in the swirling snow. Just then Anna had a thought.

"Let's call The Lovin' Oven," she suggested.

"Mom, that's all the way across town, and it's late afternoon on Christmas Eve. They are probably closed already for the holiday," Sheila said. "Besides, we're in the middle of a blizzard."

"Honey, desperate times call for desperate measures."

Sheila pulled out her cell phone and called the bakery in Lancaster, a suburb southeast of Dallas, about twenty-five miles from the bakery with no pies.

"Merry Christmas from The Lovin' Oven; how can I help you?" said the voice on the line.

Sheila could barely get the words out, she was so frantic: "I'm the dessert person for two Christmas parties, and another place messed up my order. I have no pies for Christmas. I need pies. I know it's late, but please, do you have any at all?"

"Let me check, darlin'," said the Lovin' Oven lady.

Snow coated the windshield. The wind blasted. Sheila and Anna waited for the pie report. When it came, Sheila could not believe her ears.

"Please, say that again?" she said with a lump in her throat and tears in her eyes. "I'm not sure I heard you right."

"Sugar, like I said, we have seven pies left: Two pumpkin. Two pecan. Two chess. And one lemon meringue."

It was the Miracle of the Christmas Pies!

The Lovin' Oven had *exactly* the pies Sheila had ordered from the other bakery.

"Please, please, don't close," Sheila said. "We'll be there as quickly as we can make it!"

"We'll wait for you, darlin'; drive careful!"

A half hour later, Sheila and Anna slushed into The Lovin' Oven. The employees cheered when they walked in. Seven pies were boxed and ready for them on the counter.

"Merry Christmas!" the bakery workers said.

Wait! There's more.

The Lovin' Oven was about to close for the holidays. So the staff not only handed over the seven perfect pies, but they also cleaned out their display cases and gave Sheila and Anna a giant party cake big enough to feed thirty people—and two dozen Christmas cookies!!

"Thank you, Lord," Sheila prayed on the way home. "Once again, you overdelivered!"

THE PERFECT ENDING!

I think the lesson in these stories of "imperfect" Christmases is that most of them turned out to be perfect in unexpected ways. So many times what may not seem to be the perfect situation turns out to be better than we'd ever dreamed. I hope you have your perfect Christmas, but if it doesn't seem to be that way at first, keep in mind that you don't know what God has in store. He may still be wrapping the perfect Christmas for you to open later!

CHAPTER FOUR

Our Mother's Christmas China

Every time we visit my mother's home and I see the china cabinet in her dining room, I think of a Christmas past that was one of the most difficult my family has ever experienced. Yet when we look back on that holiday season, we are all grateful, because the challenges brought us even closer as a family and we learned some important lessons on always staying in faith and believing in God's plan for us.

My mother's china cabinet holds a beautiful set of dishes my brother and sisters and I bought for her as a Christmas gift in 1981. She'd been wanting a nice set of dinnerware to use at family gatherings for quite a while, so that was one reason we decided to chip in and buy it for her. Still, there was a deeper meaning to this gift. We gave the fancy china to our mother as a symbol of our belief that she would be with us for a long, long time—long enough to wear the fancy patterns right off those cups, plates, and saucers.

You see, our mother fell sick—the worst she'd ever been—in that winter of 1981. Other than a childhood bout with polio, which she totally recovered from, our mother had always been healthy and just the most active and durable person. Paul says he'd always thought of her as being "made of nails."

Mother was only forty-eight years old and looking forward to life with an empty nest by that time. Paul and I were away at school, and both Lisa and Tamara were living on their own too. Only our youngest sister, April, was at home then, and she was in high school, so things had quieted down. My parents were beginning to make plans for traveling more often, visiting their favorite places together.

They were on a trip to Tulsa, Oklahoma, when my mother first felt sick. They'd been invited to an event at Oral Roberts University. Paul was a medical student there, in his fourth year, and I was a freshman undergrad, so they also were looking forward to see-ing us—well, at least *me*!

My parents had a great time on the first day of their visit. That night, though, Mom came down with the chills and a fever. The symptoms grew more severe over the next few days and weeks. She felt exhausted but couldn't sleep. She became so jaundiced that her doctors asked if she'd been eating a lot of carrots or squash. She suffered night sweats and sharp pains in her abdomen, like she was being stabbed.

Our mother is not a complainer. She tried to keep up with the housework and to attend church services, but she'd grown so weak that one Sunday she didn't have the strength to stand after kneeling at a service. She had to brace herself with a chair to rise up. Mom was a registered nurse, so she knew something serious was wrong. As the holiday season approached, she went to a Houston doctor. He asked her to check into the hospital for tests. She expected to be there two or three days. They kept her for twenty.

Initially, doctors thought she'd picked up some exotic bug on one of her mission trips to India with my father. They gave her all sorts of medications, which only made her feel depressed, nauseous, and fuzzy headed. Then their tests found no sign of bacteria, amoebas, or parasites, ruling out those diagnoses.

That was a relief because the treatment was making her even sicker, but doctors still didn't know what was causing her fever and pain. Finally they decided to have her blood checked to see if there were any signs of cancer, even though one doctor said he was sure there wasn't any malignancy in her body.

This was the first mention of cancer in any way, and it knocked her for a loop. She had long thanked God for sparing her of serious illness, and at first my mother refused to let anyone even use the word *cancer* in her presence. She didn't want to give it any power over her.

"I will not have cancer!" she insisted.

But then two weeks before Christmas, a doctor stopped my father in the hall at the hospital and told him that tests had found metastatic cancer in my mother's liver. He said they would continue to treat her but that it was likely she would live only a few more weeks. The liver is the filter for our blood supply, so when cancer reaches the liver, it finds a rich source of nutrients and grows rapidly. Chemotherapy is not considered effective in such cases, the doctor said.

My father was stunned. First Dad called my brother, Paul, who was by then doing his fourth-year medical rotation at Hermann Hospital just a half mile or so away from the hospital where my mother was staying. Our father told Paul that he should come and be with Mom.

At the time Paul was treating several patients with cancer and had been doing a lot of research. He was well aware of the fact that people with liver cancer usually did not live very long. When our father called and told him about his mother's cancer, Paul went from being a doctor in training who tried to stay professionally detached from his cancer patients to being a son suddenly overwhelmed emotionally with concern for his mother diagnosed with the same disease.

My brother found himself running all the way to the hospital. When he reached her floor and saw our father in the hallway outside her room, Paul lost it. He broke down in tears right there.

This was the first time any of us kids had to face

the thought of losing one of our parents. The prospect of our mother's dying seemed impossible to contemplate, and somehow having this occur over the holidays seemed all the more disorienting. The Christmas holidays had always been such a happy time for our family, as for most. Even as our lives took us away from our family home, we always came together this time of year to share our blessings and to be grateful for all we had.

At one point, I remember thinking it was unfair that our mother was forced to deal with this over such a special time of the year, but then another thought hit me: *This is the best time, because we are all coming together. We'll be there for her to support her and show our faith and love. We can ease her mind and take it off her illness by focusing instead on the birth of Jesus and all of God's blessings we look forward to.*

Just the thought of our giving strength to our mother was strange, because she'd always been the highly efficient, tireless motor who powered us through childhood and kept us going beyond it, which made it all the more difficult to see her struggle that Christmas of 1981.

I was at school and preparing to come home for the holidays when Paul called to tell me Mom was sick. He didn't elaborate or let on how serious it was. I thought it was strange that she was sick at all, because she'd always been the healthiest person in our family. I could not remember her ever being bedridden or in the hospital. I hardly ever remember a time when she even sat down while we were kids. She was always working in the house, in the yard, at school, or at the church.

"Does she have the flu or something?" I asked Paul.

"No, Joel, she's really sick; I'll tell you more when you get home," Paul said.

Dad picked me up at the airport, and to be honest, at first I thought he was sick too. He looked like he'd aged thirty years since I'd seen him at Thanksgiving. He moved in slow motion, as though he were carrying a burden so heavy that the weight of it might take him down any minute.

"Joel, your mother has a serious illness, and she may not make it," was all he said in answer to my questions.

My brother and sisters were assembled around the

fireplace in the family room when we arrived home. My father told us about the cancer and how long doctors said she had. Then we prayed.

Some of the Christmas decorations were up already, adding to the surreal nature of the somber moment. I reminded myself that God had a plan and that we should make the most of this holiday to show our love for our mother and for one another. I also expressed gratitude for the many, many Christmases we'd had that were joyous and without turmoil.

Dad told us that we had to trust in our God and stand fast in faith and pray with our mother against this challenge. There was no doubt that she was a strong woman, but none of us had any idea just how determined our mother would prove to be when standing against this deadly threat.

THE FIGHT

Metastatic cancer cells are those that have spread from a tumor to other parts of the body. Doctors said they could not find the tumor that was the source of the metastatic cells found in our mother's liver, which was unusual. They wanted to do exploratory surgery to find the tumor, but my father and mother decided that she should come home first to rest and pray about what to do.

Mom grew up in Baytown, Texas, as an only child, so she really enjoyed having all of her children around her during the holidays. She let us know right away that she wanted this to be a regular Christmas. I can't remember her even acting sick the entire time I was home on break. I'm sure she never took a nap or complained, even though she weighed only eighty-nine pounds and felt terrible.

She'd never been much for the commercial trimmings of the holiday. Her emphasis was always on the birthday of Jesus. When we were little and living out near Hobby Airport, one Christmas she made a holiday sign out of plastic place mats and tinfoil letters that read "Happy Birthday, Jesus" and put little lights around it. She put it up in the bay window that faced the street, and Paul said his friends teased him about it. He complained about it then but later realized how that sign was just another way in which our mother courageously and boldly declared her faith and her belief in what Christmas is all about.

Mom didn't make much of the whole Santa Claus thing either as we were growing up. She and Dad stored our presents in a closet. She told us not to peek and warned that if we did, she might not know but Jesus would! Mom liked to read family devotions to us at dinnertime, but she had a tough audience. Paul would make faces that made the rest of us laugh. Paul's face still makes me laugh to this day! It's a brother thing.

My sister Lisa had recovered from a childhood illness that was supposed to cripple her for life, and since then my parents put a great deal of faith in the healing power of prayer and miracles. So they decided to forgo any other tests or treatments for Mom, since doctors said she was terminal and any further treatments were likely to make her feel worse. Instead, my mother decided she was going to fight the cancer with all the prayers and faith she could muster.

Lisa had just graduated from college. She came home to be with Mom and encourage her. Like the rest of us, she couldn't fathom our mother being sick, let alone dying. We'd seen so many miracles—Lisa had lived one—so we all just focused on praying and thanking God for letting Mom live.

April had already seen more of Mom's fight than the rest of us who were no longer living with her. Early on, she remembers being shocked one day because Mom "looked like death."

"Still, I never thought she wouldn't be there for that Christmas. Dad said we were going to pray for a miracle and get one, and I believed him," April recalled. "I actually have good memories of that holiday because Mama was back home after being in the hospital so long. I could tell she didn't feel very well, but she had such deep-down faith, and we were all so happy to have everyone home for the holiday. It was so quiet with them all gone, especially Joel!"

We tried to have a normal Christmas to cheer up our mother. We teased and laughed just like always. Mom believes in the healing power of laughter; in fact, she admits that she watched more funny movies and cartoons than she ever had before during this period, trying to keep her spirits up. We supported her over the holiday, and you can believe there were a lot of prayers going out every hour of the day from our family, friends, and members of the church. My mother's illness could have cast a cloud over that holiday season, but her spirit and determination were so strong that we drew strength from her and from one another.

We'd already been planning to give her the china set for Christmas when we learned of the terminal cancer diagnosis. Rather than cancel our plan, we decided to go ahead. Lisa was a strong advocate for buying the china. She felt such a gift would assure our mother that we believed she would overcome the cancer and be with us for many family dinners and holidays to come.

Lisa, who has always been sort of the assistant mother and chief organizer among the kids in our family, took April shopping and found the china pattern Mom had once admired. There was only one problem: they didn't have as many pieces as we needed if everyone was coming to dinner. The salesperson said it might take another six weeks to complete the set.

On Christmas Day, we all gathered at our parents' home to exchange gifts and have dinner together.

OUR MOTHER'S CHRISTMAS CHINA

We all did our best to be upbeat. Mom wasn't feeling well, but she kept a smile on her face. She hugged every one of her kids and grandkids a little longer than usual. We tried to make her laugh and to let her know we loved her.

After Mom opened the china set on Christmas Day and thanked us for the beautiful gift, Lisa told her that it would take a month or so for all the pieces to be delivered. I noticed a look of sadness and doubt flash across her face. She admitted later that she'd been thinking, *I might not be here that long.*

Sensing her moment of doubt, we encouraged her, saying that we planned on wearing out that china with many years of holiday meals and family gatherings. My mother rarely allowed doubt and fear to enter her mind. She believed the enemy was trying to take away her hope and faith on that Christmas Day. She felt most of that holiday season was spent in a minute-by-minute battle with the enemy, fighting for her life and her soul.

She's told the story of her healing many times and in her own writing. My mother basically decided that her healing was a matter between her and God. She was determined to believe that God would spare her, so she refused to act sick. She refused to stay in bed or even to take a nap. Instead, she dressed like normal and went about her day, sleeping only at the normal time.

She'd read in the Bible (Matthew 18:19 NASB) that Jesus said: "If two of you agree on earth about anything that they may ask, it shall be done for them by My Father who is in heaven." So, she enlisted my father to join her in taking authority over the Enemy.

"We must agree that God is going to heal me and make me whole," she said.

Our mother believes that her healing began with those prayers on the day after she returned from the hospital. Most of the symptoms lingered for a long time, and she often felt it would be easier to give up, but each night, she prayed and promised that if she lived, she would declare the works of the Lord. She also examined her heart and decided she needed to forgive and ask forgiveness from several people. She wrote them each letters and welcomed their responses.

Mom knew staying home would just make her feel sick and sorry for herself, so despite her weakness and pain over that holiday, she drove to hospitals around the area or visited others in need and prayed with them. She flooded God with prayers. She prayed when driving, while walking to the mailbox, and while cooking meals, always asking for God's help and healing.

We all prayed for her, and every day when we saw her, we would tell her that she was healed. We wanted to give her as much positive support as we could. Still, she had pain, and fear would grip her from time to time. She fought it with everything she had. The worse she felt, the more Scripture she'd read and the more she'd pray. She made a list of forty healing scriptures that she felt applied to her health, and then she repeated them over and over and over again to encourage herself.

If you haven't noticed, my mother is a woman of fierce determination. Her decision to fight her cancer inspired many people. Some came to Houston to pray for her and tell her how they'd been diagnosed with cancer and other illnesses but made it through.

She fought to stay positive but to always be truthful too, so when someone asked her how she felt, my mother wouldn't lie if she was hurting. Instead, she would say: "I am blessed of the Lord."

One day during her fight with cancer, she and my dad returned home from church. My father was hanging up his jacket when he heard the pages of his King James Bible turning on a bedside table. There were no fans on. None of the windows were open. Yet, he found the Bible turned to Psalm 105:37: "He brought them forth also with silver and gold: and there was not one feeble person among their tribes."

My parents took great encouragement from that. Mom told us that she was not about to appear feeble or weak, so we used it against her. One day we were all hanging around the house, when she asked for help moving a small piece of furniture. We told her she was well enough to do it herself. That irritated her, but she did it and afterwards felt good that she had.

My mother never returned to that hospital bed. The Christmas of 1981 was not an easy one for her, or for those who love her. We knew she was hurting, and we tried to strike a balance between respecting her illness and encouraging her fight against it. The china set became a symbol of that approach, which is why even today when I see it in her cabinet, I say a prayer of thanks to God for letting us keep our beloved mother a while longer.

THE VICTORY

Today she is still going strong, and we look forward to many more holidays, using that china set. I can hardly believe we've had those dishes now for nearly thirty years. The diagnosis of liver cancer in my mother was checked and rechecked by a number of pathologists, radiologists, and internists, and they all reached the same conclusion as did two medical laboratories. In recent years, Mom has had many tests, and they've always come back negative for cancer.

My mother's physician classified her recovery as "a supernatural healing in response to prayer."

The physician noted that doctors are finding more and more that a positive attitude can assist healing; in fact, it can literally change white-blood-cell counts in the body, activating the body's natural defenses against cancer and other diseases.

To this day, our mother reads healing scriptures each morning before leaving the house, including this one from Jeremiah 30:17 (NKJV): "I will restore health to you, and heal you of your wounds."

We'd like to think the china set we gave her helped cure our mother's cancer by keeping her focused on a long life through that difficult holiday season in 1981. As much as we'd like to take credit, we believe God answered our prayers and those of our mother and father and their friends and supporters. All the credit is His. We are grateful for each day He gives us with her, but we are especially grateful at Christmas when we sit down to dinner with those cups, plates, and saucers we gave our mother. The china setting helps us to appreciate the day even more because it serves as a reminder of the holiday season years ago, when we were concerned we would have her no more.

I encourage you to be grateful for the time you have with your family members, not just over the holidays but every day of the year. Make the most of each moment and thank God for his continued blessings.

CHAPTER FIVE

Christmas at Meemaw's House

M y childhood Christmases mostly were spent
with all my family at home in Humble, Texas,
but Victoria and her family traveled from Houston
nearly every Christmas season to visit her mother's
parents at their grand old hilltop home in Columbus,
Georgia. Each holiday season, Victoria, her brother
Don Jr., and her parents, Don Sr. and Georgine, packed
the family car with luggage and gifts and departed
at first light for the seven-hundred-mile trip. Victoria
and Don, who is four years older, usually took pillows and slept for the first few hundred miles. Then
they'd wake up, read, play games, or simply enjoy the
sights as they passed along the Gulf Coast and then

up through small Southern towns like Opelousas, Bogalusa, and Poplarville.

Victoria and her brother enjoyed tormenting their parents with requests for updates at regular intervals:

"Are we there yet, Daddy?"

"Mommy, how much longer?"

Then there were the usual sibling backseat battles: Don's legs would stray into Victoria's territory. Her reading material might spill onto Don's section of the seat. Fortunately for all, there were outside distractions on this long journey. Victoria and her brother loved checking out the Christmas decorations in each small town as they passed through. They'd made this trip so often that they remembered which towns had a Santa House on the square, manger scene on the courthouse lawn, or Christmas tree in the park. Their mother's favorite roadside attractions were the small-town antique stores, which sometimes lured her out of the car and through their doors, providing a break in the trip and sometimes adding cargo too.

With "Jingle Bells" and other holiday tunes on the radio and the passing parade of Christmas decorations, the long drive served to pump Victoria and her brother full of excitement and anticipation for the birthday of Jesus, the arrival of Santa, and the week-long visit with their grandparents, aunts, uncles, and favorite cousins.

They'd be driving in moonlight by the time their car crossed the border of Alabama and into Georgia. Columbus awaited just on the other side of the Chattahoochee River. The scenic city of graceful old mansions dating back to the Civil War sits in the beautiful river valley. Victoria and Don's excitement peaked when the family car climbed a large hill overlooking their grandparents' stately 1800s home, aglow with Christmas lights and the warmth of a loving family assembled to greet them.

As they pulled up to the driveway, their raven-haired grandfather, George, would always be there to greet them, striding down the steps of the side porch with a wide welcoming grin. "I saw you a-coming over the hill," he said each time. Their grandfather would crouch down, arms extended, inviting Victoria and Don to scramble into his embrace. Hugs were welcome, but what he wanted most were kisses on his cheek.

"Give me some jaw-sugar!" he'd demand.

Victoria and Don always complied.

About that time, Victoria's grandmother would appear through the back door, hurrying down the steps toward them, but always headed toward her daughter first. She would hug Georgine, kiss her face, and then look adoringly into her eyes. At that moment, the only thing that mattered to Eula Mae Blalock was that her daughter was home.

Victoria would wait politely for her own first moment with the matriarch of the family, known to all the grandchildren as Meemaw. A Southern beauty with a quick wit and sharp business mind, Eula Mae Blalock had grown up in the genteel port city of Savannah. Relatives in Columbus often say Victoria reminds them of her maternal grandmother, who was a proper, faith-filled lady but very warm and fun to be around. Georgine says Victoria also inherited her grandmother's wonderful laugh, and I'm grateful for that because she surely has a great one.

As the daughter of a prosperous grocer who owned a small chain of stores, Meemaw came from a long line of merchants and entrepreneurs. She often entranced her grandchildren with stories of their ancestors, particularly Victoria's great-grandfather who had owned a grocery and general store. One of her favorite stories told of his concern for the townspeople hit hardest during the Depression years.

Meemaw's father kept two sets of credit books for his customers. The first book was for those who would buy their groceries on credit and then faithfully pay their bills at the end of each month. The other set of books was for those customers who had trouble making the monthly payment. The grocer told his employees to record each purchase, but to never let on that those customers probably won't pay.

"We don't want their children to think their parents are taking charity," he always said. Meemaw's eyes often filled with tears when she told that story. Then she'd whisper, "I so miss my father."

We all have our own interpretations of the Christmas spirit. Victoria and Don grew up in a strong Christian family that read Scripture and prayed each day.

If you ask Victoria's mother or any of Victoria's aunts or uncles about Eula Mae Blalock, they always start the conversation by telling you what a great mother she was. Then, they'll most likely talk about her powerful faith in God and her caring ways. Victoria's mother, Georgine, was one of nine children, and she often said that her mother made each of them feel like her favorite.

"She had that gift," Georgine says. "She doted on her children, treating each one like he or she were the only child she had. Every week she made a new dress for me and hung it on my bedroom door. She would buy different fabrics for each of my sisters' dresses so that we all looked special. I always knew she had chosen the fabric for my dress especially for me."

Victoria's grandfather worked as a civilian engineer at Fort Benning, just outside Columbus, while Eula Mae took care of the children until they were off and on their own.

Then Meemaw started by buying small homes, fixing them up, and then renting them to soldiers and their families who were stationed at the nearby military base. She might sell one house and buy two more or even trade houses with local builders. Soon she was buying larger homes, splitting them into duplexes, and renting them to multiple families. By the time Victoria's mother married, her grandmother owned several properties, all of which were generating a profit. By the early 1960s, Meemaw was able to achieve her dream of buying a home big enough for all of her children and grandchildren—the beautiful Victorian house that sat on a large property known to locals as the old Mooney estate.

At a time in life when many couples are downsizing, Eula Mae and George Blalock bought one of the biggest properties they'd ever owned. The old Mooney estate included acres of beautiful rolling hills covered in wildflowers. The grand old home also was surrounded by thick stands of pines that secluded Mooney Lake.

Still, the home's most important features for Eula Mae were its five bedrooms and baths, oversize living and dining rooms, and big country kitchen that could accommodate visiting family during the holidays. This was the home where Victoria and her many relatives accumulated cherished Christmas memories, and it is where they learned the depth of their family's faith and caring.

"There was just something about Meemaw's house," Victoria told me. "It was warm, peaceful, and safe, and it was filled with love. I always thought I could feel the presence of God there."

HOLIDAY HOME

Victoria recalls that her grandmother always seemed to be at peace there. Meemaw loved the Christmas season more than any other time of year and often said that her house was her "gift from God" because it allowed her to have so many of her children and grandchildren together for the holidays.

Eula Mae Blalock was a woman of extraordinary faith, a strong Christian. Soon after she and George moved onto the property, she carved out a little place at the edge of the trees behind the house where she would go off to pray quietly every morning for twenty minutes or so. She would get up early each morning and walk from the back porch, through her garden, and then another thirty yards or so to the tree line where she'd drop to her knees in the grass and pray for her children and grandchildren, asking God to bless them.

Victoria and her cousins called that special place near the trees "Meemaw's altar," and they always treated the shaded spot as a blessed place. Victoria remembers mornings when she would wake up early and go looking for her grandmother. She'd venture into the big country kitchen drawn by the smells of bacon and biscuits, only to find Meemaw standing at the stove in her housecoat, her knees still moist from dew after her morning prayer. From time to time, Victoria would slip out the back door and, like her grandmother, walk through the garden, cross the yard, and pray at her grandmother's altar. She often wondered if her grandmother was watching, secretly hoping she was.

By the second or third day of their annual holiday visit, Victoria and Don found the table a little more crowded as other members of the family piled into the house. Eventually, they were joined at their grandparents' place by thirty or more aunts, uncles, and cousins. The arrival of each family brought more presents under the massive Christmas tree worthy of Rockefeller Center. Each year a choice fir tree was cut from the surrounding woods by their cousin Clyde Wolf Jr. Junior would chop down the mighty tree and drag it hundreds of yards through the thick undergrowth and build a stand for it. Then he and his grandfather would wrestle it up the back porch, through the kitchen and dining room, and finally into the living room where it was adorned with Christmas decorations and served as the centerpiece of all holiday activities.

On the fun-filled days that followed, the adults huddled to make preparations and to discuss religion and politics—always favorite topics—while the young girls danced and played games and the boys hunted, staged mock battles, and of course conspired to torment the girls in every possible way.

CHRISTMAS BLAST

One memorable Christmas visit, Don Jr. somehow convinced his father to buy fireworks for him and his co-conspirator cousins. After they grew bored with blowing up paper cups and bombing unsuspecting woodland creatures, the boys turned to a fresh target.

Victoria's cousin, Debra, one of her favorites, had received an Easy-Bake Oven as an early Christmas present. She made the mistake of bringing it to Meemaw's house and leaving it outside on a picnic table, within reach of the boys in the bomb squad. Their first effort at cooking up an Easy-Bake blast involved tying together a small string of firecrackers and placing them inside the oven.

The resulting chain of explosions was loud, but apparently not loud enough.

"Well, that was no big deal," Junior exclaimed. "Let's try this!"

The oldest-ranking cousin on the bomb squad then produced a cherry bomb, which is basically a big wad of gunpowder wrapped up to look like an innocent piece of fruit. Cherry bombs are now illegal in most states, for good reason.

Junior placed the cherry bomb inside the Easy-Bake Oven. Witnesses would later testify under intense questioning that his all-too-willing accomplice, Don

Jr., then lit the fuse and slammed the door shut before joining his cousins in a scramble for cover.

The cherry bomb then did exactly what cherry bombs ignited in confined spaces do. It blew poor Cousin Debra's brand-new Easy-Bake Oven to smithereens!

Grandparents, parents, aunts, and uncles had hardly noticed previous firecracker explosions due to their distance from the mischief and the din of their own conversations. The cherry bomb, they heard.

Adults came pouring out of the Victorian doors in fear of lost body parts among their young. Instead, they found the charred remnants of the Easy-Bake Oven and a group of boys stricken with the certainty that they were about to be taken to the woodshed.

The girl cousins followed the crowd and, upon arriving at the scene of the crime, surrounded Cousin Debra.

"My oven! Where's my oven? What did you do to my oven?"

Victoria's brother is known for his gift of gab, but the gift evaded him in that particular moment. Junior also took the Fifth, choosing to remain silent rather

than incriminate himself. It was left up to one of the younger male cousins to take them down.

"It was Clyde's idea and Don lit it!"

The Easy-Bake bombers were ordered to replace their cousin's Christmas present and to save their fireworks for the Fourth of July.

THE BIG DAY

The holiday celebration began in earnest on Christmas Eve when Meemaw and the other women prepared a traditional Southern Christmas meal. By noon on Christmas Day, the house would be filled with the aroma of roast turkey, cornbread dressing, and Aunt Lois's sugary sweet potatoes. Come dinnertime, the adults were seated at the long dining-room table, while the younger generation jockeyed for position at one or more of the designated kids' tables set up in the adjoining living room.

Once everyone was seated, the women brought out platters and bowls of mouthwatering food.

The final dish produced each Christmas Eve was

Meemaw's own homemade cornbread. Then all voices were hushed so that one of the uncles could lead the family in saying the blessing. He would thank God that they were all together and that everyone was healthy, and then he would ask God to bless the food.

Quietly Meemaw thanked God for the house too.

After loading up on dinner and clearing the dishes, all parties adjourned to the back porch for more conversation and laughter. Victoria loved hearing stories from her aunts and uncles, particularly Uncle J.H., who pastored a church. Still, she basked in the great interest other family members showed in hearing about her father's important work.

It was the 1960s and the entire nation was preoccupied with America's quest to land a man on the moon. Victoria's dad, Don, was in the middle of that quest. He is a mathematician, and at the time he worked as a division chief at NASA in Houston. He had also worked with Wernher von Braun, the renowned German scientist who headed the team that designed the Saturn V rocket—the very rocket that was propelling American astronauts toward the moon.

Victoria's aunts and uncles were full of questions

about the astronauts, the space craft, and her father's involvement in the latest mission. Her father always seemed to enjoy answering their questions and discussing his challenging work. I'm grateful to have this gentle, kind, and brilliant man as a father-in-law. Our son Jonathan and daughter Alexandra are blessed to have their Grandfather Iloff's mathematical mind, and I'm especially grateful for that!

HER GRANDMOTHER'S VOICE

Late on Christmas Eve, the children would settle in on mattresses placed around the Christmas tree. Boys on one side of the living room, girls on the other. With just the Christmas-tree lights providing illumination, most of the children would give in to weariness and fall asleep after a half hour or so of chatter. Victoria usually held off, because she loved to listen to her mother, grandmother, and aunts and uncles talking around the kitchen table.

The conversation always turned to the Bible sooner or later, and Meemaw, a devoted reader of the Scrip-

tures, led the discussions. Meemaw loved the Bible and could find the right passage for any occasion. It didn't matter whether Aunt Sue was considering a new job offer or Aunt Mary had a pain in her ankle or even if Aunt Christine was buying a new house— Meemaw always had a scripture. Victoria says that even though she had gone to church all of her life, she learned more Bible scriptures eavesdropping on Meemaw's kitchen conversations than she ever did in church. Victoria loved listening to Meemaw offer her readings and thoughts on God's Word. Most nights, including Christmas Eve and Christmas Day, she fell asleep to the sound of her grandmother's soft voice.

MEMORIES OF MEEMAW

Victoria cherishes those childhood memories especially because she didn't have many years with her grandmother. Sadly, Meemaw passed away when Victoria was just twelve years old, in 1972. Her grandmother had rarely been ill. She suffered a heart attack that took her life. Doctors suspected that a bout of rheumatic fever in childhood had weakened her heart. Regardless of the cause, the entire family was devastated.

Victoria's grandfather, George, had been so close to his wife that everyone worried how he would get along without her. He was a few years older and losing his wife of so many years proved to be very hard on him. A short time after Meemaw died, George followed her to heaven.

It was a sad, sad time.

Victoria and Don lost both their Blalock grandparents in a very short time, and with them went their visits to Meemaw's house, which had been the scene of so many great vacations and holidays. It was five or six years after her grandparents had passed that Victoria and her parents returned to Columbus over the holidays to stay with relatives still in the area.

One Sunday, Victoria was riding around town in a car driven by her older cousin Joan when they decided to drive by Meemaw's house for old times' sake. They knew it had been sold after their grandparents' passing, but the girls were surprised to find a sign in the yard indicating that Meemaw's home had become a church.

They watched several people leave through the open front doors, so they figured services must be over. Then Joan turned to Victoria and said: "Do you want to go inside?"

Curiosity and maybe a force more powerful drew them into the house, which seemed so familiar yet different too. If you've ever returned to a childhood home or even your grade school, you know the feeling. In some ways the place is unchanged and you feel like you belong there, but without your old furnishings or the others who occupied it with you, there is also this sense that you are a stranger there. Yet when familiar sights, sounds, and smells wash over you, the place seems to welcome you and draw you in. Seeing your childhood bedroom with the built-in bookshelves and old pine tree outside the window or encountering the long-ago smells of your grade-school cafeteria—experiences like that can yank the covers off images and events stored deep in your brain.

Visiting places from your past can be rewarding, but also disorienting and emotional. When Victoria and Joan walked in the front door of Meemaw's house, they were carried back to every one of those family gatherings and Christmases past. They stepped through the entryway and into remembered times forever stored in the high ceilings and the opposing corners of the room: one where the world's largest Christmas tree once stood but no longer did, and in the other where an old organ had replaced Meemaw's antique piano.

The living and dining rooms where they'd laughed and played with family had been combined and set up as the worship area with an altar and pastor's podium. And while the long dining table was gone along with Meemaw's china and crystal, the place still looked much the same. Stepping back into their childhoods, the cousins suddenly were lost in time, transported back and beyond that day into years gone by.

As Victoria's gaze moved beyond the dining room, she could still see what appeared to be a kitchen. Slowly she moved closer and looked through the doorway. It seemed familiar, yet different. The old refrigerator had been replaced with a new one, and on the countertop sat a large coffeemaker in place of Meemaw's wooden flour bowl. But still that kitchen, where she had helped her grandmother make biscuits, triggered memories in bursts so urgent that both she and Joan felt dizzy. Neither said a word at first; the two of them were so overwhelmed that they just melted into the folding chairs that served as pews. Victoria closed her eyes and sat silently as if listening for her Meemaw's voice softly quoting Scripture.

At first they hardly noticed the members of the church gathering for the next service in the front of the room. The church members studied these two young strangers who'd walked into their house of worship. Theirs was a small church with perhaps seventy-five members, so they knew that Victoria and Joan were visitors. Still, they let them be. The young ladies were so somber that they seemed to be in need of prayer.

Joan began crying first, weeping quietly. Victoria heard her and saw the tears, and she finally lost it too. They were overcome with lingering grief for their grandparents and the full realization that this house of wonderful memories was no longer part of their lives.

As Joan and Victoria let go, five or six women from

the congregation rose from their seats and gathered around the young ladies, consoling them, being kind. Then the pastor, who lived upstairs, came in and began asking gently if the visitors needed to repent of their sins and receive Christ. The pastor was confused; he thought Victoria and Joan had been drawn into the church by a crisis of some sort, which is understandable given their emotional state.

When Joan realized what the pastor and his flock were thinking, she stifled her tears long enough to explain: "I'm sorry for interrupting your services. This was our grandparents' home, and this is the first time we've been back since they passed," she said. "We're sorry, we just got carried away by our memories of all the love and good times we had here."

Her words transformed the mood in the room. No longer concerned for their souls and well-being, the church members welcomed and encouraged them to stay and look around as long as they wanted. One lady, who may have been the pastor's wife, pulled Joan aside and told her: "When we first looked at this place and considered it for our house of prayer, we sensed that it had been a loving Christian home and a place where God was welcomed and had a strong presence."

Well, that nearly set Victoria and Joan to crying again, but they held it together. Joan assured the pastor and his flock that their grandparents and especially her grandmother had been strong Christians. She even pointed out the place where "Meemaw's altar" had been at the edge of the trees surrounding the house.

Their hosts seemed reassured and grateful to hear that. Victoria recalls that she suddenly felt as though they'd joined a revival meeting, with the pastor and his church members praising the Lord and calling blessings upon her and Joan, their grandparents, and all their family members here and gone.

The pastor noted that God must have had a plan for the old house, washing it first with the love of a Christian family, celebrating the birth of His son for many years, and then turning it into the Father's home, a welcoming place of abiding faith and everlasting love.

Victoria and Joan thanked the pastor and his flock and returned to their car. A shared sense of peace flowed over the cousins. Their final visit to Meemaw's house had given them closure. They were glad they'd stopped by, and they were comforted to know that a place filled with so much love, so much faith, and so many holiday memories now had God in permanent residence.

Their hearts told them that their loving Meemaw would be glad as well.

CHAPTER SIX

A White Christmas in Mexico

✧

Marcos Witt's parents were missionaries who could not afford many expensive Christmas presents when he and his brothers and sisters were growing up. They spent most of their funds trying to spread the Word of God. Yet over the years they gave Marcos certain special gifts that opened up new worlds to him, forever changing his life and impacting those of millions around the world.

"Our gifts were never huge or spectacular, but we did get stocking stuffers and at least one big gift each year with some smaller gifts from our parents and other relatives," Marcos said. "My best gift, I'd have to say, was my first guitar."

Marcos was just ten years old on the Christmas Day he found the Three Pines guitar under the tree. It was not an expensive guitar but a good solid instrument. He'd wanted one because in Durango, the Mexican mountain valley town where they lived, "every other person you met played the guitar."

Most of the music he'd heard was in church, of course, so Marcos began by learning to play those songs. His was not the usual music-practice room. The missionaries' son practiced while riding in the back of his father's pickup as they traveled to the remote villages where his parents had planted churches. There, under a camper top in the back of the pickup bouncing on rutted roads, the boy and his friends made music that would one day fill concert halls.

"Usually there were six or seven of us back there with two or three guitars. One guy could really play, and we learned the chords from him. I learned many songs on my Christmas guitar in the back of that pickup," Marcos recalls.

Despite the rough ride and hot, cramped quarters, he learned well. A few years ago Marcos recorded a collection of those songs mastered in the pickup.

He called it *Recordando Otra Vez,* or *Remembering Once Again.* The album received the 2004 Latin Grammy Award as the best Spanish-language Christian album of the year.

In fact, Marcos has won four Latin Grammy Awards and sold more than ten million copies of his Christian music CDs and DVDs around the world. Today, hundreds of thousands of people attend his concerts.

My friend Marcos, who is pastor for the large Spanish congregation at Lakewood Church, says that first guitar was the catalyst for a musical career that has taken him all over the world and allowed him to express his faith to millions of people.

Just as God's first Christmas gift to us, His son, gave rise to faith, hope, and love around the world, Marcos's parents' gift of his first guitar gave rise to musical talents that God had planted in Marcos.

WHITE CHRISTMAS SOUTH OF THE BORDER

Sometimes a person can even be blessed by a snowstorm, in Mexico. You probably have never thought of Mexico having white Christmases. They are rare, but they've occurred. Marcos was four years old when a winter storm hit Durango and buried it in snow over the Christmas holidays in 1966.

"It started raining and sleeting as we came home from Sunday service on Christmas Eve, and then around midnight it began snowing, and snowing hard, which was really unusual," Marcos said. "We were already in bed, and my mother woke us up because we'd never seen snow. There was a single street light on, and it was so quiet with the snow falling on the pine trees and no traffic sounds that it felt like the world had stopped. We sat with our noses glued to the window watching the strange white flakes come down just in time for Christmas."

Nola had often told her children that "White Christmas" was the favorite song of her mother, who had grown up in Mississippi and didn't get to see much snow on Christmas, which is why she loved the song so much. The magic of that snowy Christmas Eve night in the mountains of Mexico made it a special song for Marcos too. Think of that small boy, his face pressed against the window, seeing snow for the first time on the eve of the birthday of Jesus. Something was planted in his heart that night, something that came out through his music many years later in a place far removed from that isolated mountain town south of the border.

"I'd always wanted to record 'White Christmas' as part of an album of special Christmas songs performed with a live symphony," Marcos said. "Then in 2003 we rented Studio A at the famous Abbey Road Studios in London, where the Beatles recorded. We brought in members of the London Symphony, an eighty-piece orchestra, and recorded the Christmas album in that huge studio. It was July, but one of the producers put up a Christmas tree with decorations."

All of those great musicians recorded many songs in that session, but there was only one song done in just one take because everyone in the studio seemed to be filled with joy. Can you guess which song that was?

"I'll never forget recording 'White Christmas' ['Blanca Navidad'] that day. We performed it in one cut from beginning to end, no overdubs, no going back to clean it up," Marcos said. "I was inspired, and so were the members of the orchestra. It was such a joy-filled experience that afterward I prayed over the orchestra and thanked them for their work."

MINISTRY AND MYSTERY

God works in amazing ways. I'm reminded of that whenever I think of our family's friendship with Marcos and his family, which actually began many years ago, when Marcos and I both were just babies. And like Marcos's music career, our long relationship began with a gift.

Back in 1964 when my father met Marcos's parents, Lakewood Church was in its infancy too. The church had only about five hundred members. Jerry and Nola Witt were struggling to establish their first church in Durango, Mexico, and when they visited Lakewood, Dad called them up to speak.

Like his father before him, he worked to bring God's Word to the most remote and isolated regions of Mexico by flying a small plane over far-flung villages and dropping copies of the Gospel of John in Spanish. He told the Lakewood congregation that his dream was to plant Christian churches throughout Mexico, but first they needed a base of operations where they could have their own church, a Bible school, and a campground. Their goal was to train local pastors to spread the Word of God. Jerry also said he needed to buy a piece of property in Durango, Mexico, where they could build their operations base.

That night an offering was received from the congregation that gave Jerry $600, helping him and Nola to establish a missionary effort that has continued ever since. Sadly, Jerry Witt did not live to see the seeds he planted grow and flourish. Just a few months after he and Nola came to Lakewood, Jerry died when their plane crashed into a mountain canyon on April 8, 1964. He and a member of his congregation had just dropped three thousand pamphlets printed with the Spanish translation of the Gospel of John on several villages in a remote mountain valley.

This was a tragic event, but this amazing, resilient family is still writing its story, and there is great joy in it too. Nola found herself a widow with three young boys—Marcos, Jerry, and Felipe—in a foreign country. At the time, Nola spoke very little Spanish. Yet, she knew Jerry would have wanted her to continue their work even without him.

"I was feeling more and more that the Lord wanted me to remain in the wreckage of my life and rebuild on the same spot," she wrote in her memoir, *The Foolishness of God*.

You can imagine the weight on her shoulders and the fears in her heart. She felt unprepared for the responsibilities and the challenges. She trusted God but could not understand why He had chosen to leave her alone and in charge of this important mission. She felt crushed under the weight of it all: the responsibility, the grief, the loneliness. Her heart leaped every time a plane flew over because that had always been the first sign that her husband was coming home from past missions.

If Nola had any doubt that God was guiding her life, her faith was fully restored with the arrival of Frank Warren, whom she fondly remembers today as "the most eligible Christian bachelor west of the Mississippi." Three years after Jerry's death, Frank visited Nola's mission in Durango. He was with her brother and a group of evangelists looking to build churches in Mexico. Frank Warren also had been searching for a good Christian wife ever since he'd left military service and been saved twelve years earlier. He'd even vowed that he would not kiss another woman unless he was certain she'd be his wife.

When he kissed Nola the first time, she could tell he'd been out of practice, but he showed promise, she said. After they married, Frank Warren stepped in as her husband, as father to her sons, and as coleader of their missionary efforts. Together they had twin daughters, Jeannie and Lorie, built fifteen churches, and assisted in the creation of at least fifteen more. Something else they did, a fairly simple gesture, may have reached even more hearts and souls. You see, it was Frank and Nola who gave Marcos his first guitar for Christmas. Since he mastered that instrument so quickly, the following Christmas they gave him a mandolin.

MUSIC AND MIXING CULTURES

What they were really doing, of course, was nurturing the boy's God-given talents—and what talent he proved to have! Marcos has continued their missionary work, mostly though his songs, his speaking, and his gift of encouraging and empowering others. But it's funny because when he first began embracing Mexican traditions, it wasn't about the music. He was more interested in extending Christmas as long as possible. When their family first settled in Mexico, Nola was determined to hang on to the American traditions of Christmas. She'd even stock up on turkey, cornbread, and all the fixings when she went home to Georgia each year so that she'd have them for Christmas dinner.

Her smart middle son, though, quickly began to see the benefits of celebrating a Mexican American blend of Christmas traditions.

"To my Mexican friends it was really odd in the early years, because we couldn't open any presents on Christmas Eve. Their families opened gifts on the night before Christmas to celebrate Noche Buena [Good Night] with gifts and food," Marcos recalls. "I had to wait. My school buddies would say: 'You open gifts when? You eat your big dinner when?'"

Marcos did his best to convince his parents that they should embrace both cultures and open presents on Christmas Eve *and* Christmas Day. "My mom wasn't buying it," he said. He didn't give up, though. As a budding multicultural man, Marcos also urged his parents to adopt the Mexican holiday of El Dia de los Reyes Magos (Three Kings Day), which pretty much stretches the Christmas celebration from Christmas Day through January 6.

Once he had a wife and children of his own, Marcos began celebrating traditions from both his adopted and native countries. When he and his family lived in Mexico and now even today in their Houston home, they celebrate Noche Buena with one gift each, and then, around midnight, they have a special tamale dinner. Then, on Christmas Day, they open the rest of their gifts and have traditional American Christmas food and some from Mexico too.

"We love the idea of Good Night," Marcos said. "In Mexico, people wait until around ten or ten-thirty that night, and then they go visit friends, taking some special food as a gift and spending just five or ten minutes with them. It's a stopover sort of thing. We do that even now in the United States. We invite people over and make cookie platters for them. Every Christmas Eve, we get calls from Latino friends all over the world who still celebrate that tradition."

Marcos and his family also celebrate Three Kings Day on January 6 by going to a Latino bakery and buying a *rosca de reyes,* or kings' ring cake. It's round with a big hole in the center and decorated with dried and candied fruit like figs and cherries. You have to be careful when you eat this cake because they bake a small plastic doll into it, which represents baby Jesus. The Latino tradition is that whoever finds the baby-Jesus toy in the cake is blessed.

Marcos and his family are truly blessed with God's love. After the tragic loss of his father at such a young age, Marcos might have faced a difficult life, but his mother's faith and determination and a wonderful stepfather helped him nurture his God-given musical gifts. And it all began with a simple Christmas present, a guitar tuned to the destiny of a great musician and a great man.

THE GIFT OF
SERVICE TO OTHERS

Another of my Spanish-speaking friends, Pastor Sergio De La Mora, who leads the Cornerstone Church in San Diego, also grew up in a family with limited resources. His immigrant parents, Salvador and Solidad De La Mora, always managed to buy gifts for their six children, but they wanted their boys and girls to savor Christmas morning and to appreciate their blessings, so they had a unique family tradition.

"For me and my brothers and sisters, Christmas morning was about seeing what new toys were under the tree with our names scrawled across the top," Pastor Sergio says. "But to my parents, Christmas mornings were about creating memories that would outlast the toys we begged and pleaded for each year."

Without fail on Christmas morning, his father would hand out the gifts designated for each child. But no one was allowed to open any of their presents until all of the gifts were handed out and piled in front of each one of them.

Then the oldest child went first, opening his presents while the others watched and waited.

"In the De La Mora family, there was always an order for doing things, and Christmas was no exception," Pastor Sergio says. "With the video camera rolling, we would all sit and wait while we went down the line of kids from oldest to youngest. Unfortunately, I was the youngest!"

Sergio had to watch his brothers and sisters open their presents one by one before he could finally tear into his. He resented that at first. He even tried over the years to negotiate a reversal in the gift-opening order. But his parents refused to alter the tradition.

Looking back, Sergio says he should have grasped that they were following the Bible's promise found in

Matthew that states "the first shall be last and the last shall be first."

As a boy, Sergio had argued that doing away with the one-by-one ritual would give them all more time to play with their Christmas toys each year. Then one day years later he realized that saving time wasn't a factor in his parents' Christmas-present tradition.

"They were interested in making memories for their children, strengthening the values they had instilled in us, and, most important, keeping our hearts turned toward one another. They had passed along to us some of the greatest gifts we could ever receive—the gifts of honor, respect, deep appreciation, and delayed gratification."

It dawned on Sergio, once he became a parent himself, that because he had to wait to open his childhood Christmas gifts, he had the chance to savor and enjoy all that was happening in front of him. Suddenly he realized that there were perks to being the baby brother.

"While each one of my siblings opened gifts, none of us just sat quietly watching. No, we would all clap and get excited when someone opened that one gift they were hoping would be under the tree. Sometimes we would be even more excited for them than we were for ourselves," Sergio says. "It became just part of who we were, ingrained into our persona and character, to get excited when someone else had a dream fulfilled. Those Christmas mornings taught me how to become a dream releaser for others."

The gifts of those Christmas Day experiences were too valuable to be wrapped in a box; instead, they were put into his heart.

"Through the years I've come to realize how incredibly blessed I am to have had such wonderful parents who were rich in tradition and faith," Sergio says. "As an adult my heart is still turned toward home, and I know it's because of what my parents modeled and taught me not only during Christmas but every single day."

Conclusion

✧

I hope you have enjoyed our collection of Christmas stories from family and friends. We had so · much fun getting together and talking about our holiday memories that I recommend you do the same with your loved ones. It's amazing what you start to remember once you bring everyone together. We pulled out memories that brought with them the sights, sounds, and smells of our childhood Christmases. Mostly, though, we realized how blessed we were to have such warm and loving memories.

Our parents always emphasized to us that Christmas was about celebrating the birth of Jesus, our savior. They taught us that when we commit our lives to Him and do our best to honor God it gives more meaning not only to this holiday but to our daily lives.

They also reminded us each Christmas that while it's fun to give and receive gifts for the holidays, giving to others should be a year-round activity.

Victoria and I pray that you have many Christmases filled with joy and peace and lasting memories. Celebrate the Savior. His ultimate sacrifice is the reason we have peace, joy, and victory in our lives.

Merry Christmas and Happy New Year!

Acknowledgments

✦

Writing is usually described as a solitary process, but this book, more than any of my others, was truly a collaborative effort—and a lot of fun—as I worked with family and friends to reach back and compare memories of Christmases past. I'm grateful to my mother, Dodie, my brother, Paul, and our sisters, Lisa, Tamara, and April, for their contributions to this enjoyable process. My wife, Victoria, and her brother, Don, chipped in with their wonderful and touching childhood Christmas tales. The book was made even richer and more diverse thanks to great contributions from Don's wife Jackelyn Viera Iloff, Lakewood's pastor of Spanish Ministries Marcos Witt and his mother Nola Warren; my pastor friends Phil Munsey, Sergio

ACKNOWLEDGMENTS

De La Mora, and Matthew Barnett and Lakewood's own Gabriela Ferrel.

A special thanks to Wes Smith once again for all his hard work in pulling even more stories out of all of us and then helping me put them all together. I'm grateful also to Jan Miller Rich and Shannon Marven at DuPree Miller & Associates literary agency and to all the folks at Free Press for their enthusiasm and support.

About the Author

Joel Osteen is the senior pastor of Lakewood Church in Houston, Texas, the largest church in America. He is the author of numerous journals, devotionals, and books, including the *Hope for Today Bible* and the *New York Times* bestseller *It's Your Time*. His book *Become a Better You* has sold over two million copies to date, remaining on the *New York Times* bestseller list for five months. You can visit Joel's website at www.joelosteen.com.

PHOTO CREDITS AND CAPTIONS

Cover photo: A young Joel Osteen. *From the personal collection of Joel and Victoria Osteen.*

page iv Joel was about five years old in this portrait. *From the personal collection of Joel and Victoria Osteen.*

page xiv Joel with Rusty, the family dog, in front of the family home circa 1966. *From the personal collection of Joel and Victoria Osteen.*

page 10 Joel with his Christmas presents, including his ten-speed and his basketball gym bag. *From the personal collection of Joel and Victoria Osteen.*

page 22 Circa 1962. Top row left to right: Tamara, Father John Osteen, Paul, Mother Dodie Osteen. Bottom row: Grandfather Roy Pilgrim, Lisa, Grandmother Georgia Pilgrim. *From the personal collection of Joel and Victoria Osteen.*

page 50 Top row: Lisa and Paul. Bottom row: April, Joel, Tamara. *From the personal collection of Joel and Victoria Osteen.*

page 78 The Osteen children: top row: Lisa and Paul; bottom row: Joel, April, Tamara. *From the personal collection of Joel and Victoria Osteen.*

page 98 Victoria was two years old and Don was six years old in this photo. She is holding their black kitten. *From the personal collection of Joel and Victoria Osteen.*

page 110 Victoria found lipstick in her mother's purse and helped herself. The small mirror in her hand didn't seem to help the application process. *From the personal collection of Joel and Victoria Osteen.*

page 114 Victoria Iloff Osteen in the second grade. *From the personal collection of Joel and Victoria Osteen.*

page 124 Nola Warren and children. *From the personal collection of Nola Warren.*

Back cover photo: The Osteen family. *From the personal collection of Joel and Victoria Osteen.*